• Bartholoı

HANDY ROAI

SCOTLAND

KEY TO MAP PAGES

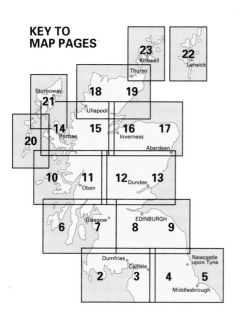

CONTENTS

2-23   Road Maps at 9 miles to 1 inch
24-25   Urban Area Maps at 4 miles to 1 inch
   24   Aberdeen, Dundee,
   25   Edinburgh, Glasgow
26-30   Index to place names
31-72   City Plans at 4 inches to 1 mile
   31   Key to City Plan Pages
32-35   Aberdeen
36-37   Index to Aberdeen
38-39   Dundee
40-41   Index to Dundee
42-49   Edinburgh
50-55   Index to Edinburgh
56-65   Glasgow
66-72   Index to Glasgow

Bartholomew Handy Road Atlas Scotland

Bartholomew
An Imprint of HarperCollins*Publishers*
77–85 Fulham Palace Road, Hammersmith, London W6 8JB

Ordnance Survey material was used in the revision of this map.
© Crown copyright (pages 32-35, 38-39, 42-49, 56-65 only)

The contents of this edition of the Bartholomew Handy Road Atlas Scotland are believed to be correct at the time of printing. Nevertheless, the publishers can accept no responsibility for errors or omissions, changes in the detail given or for any expense or loss thereby caused.

Printed by The Edinburgh Press Ltd in Scotland

ISBN 0 7028 3148 4   CDNE   HE 8105

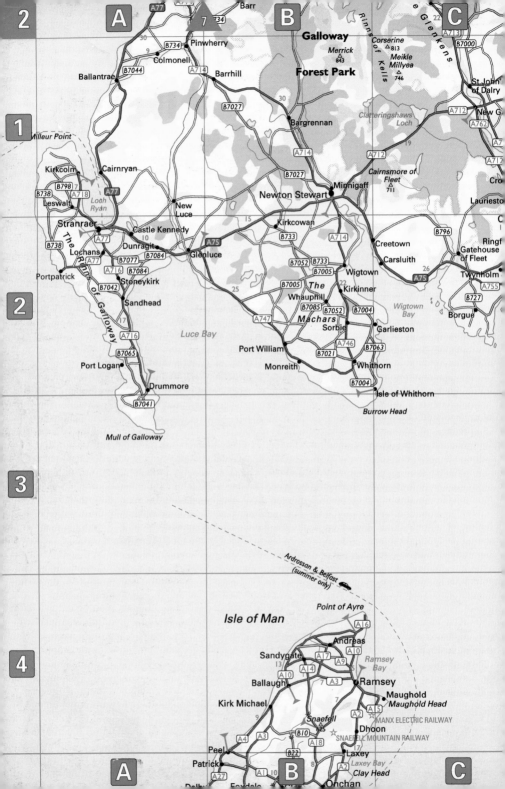

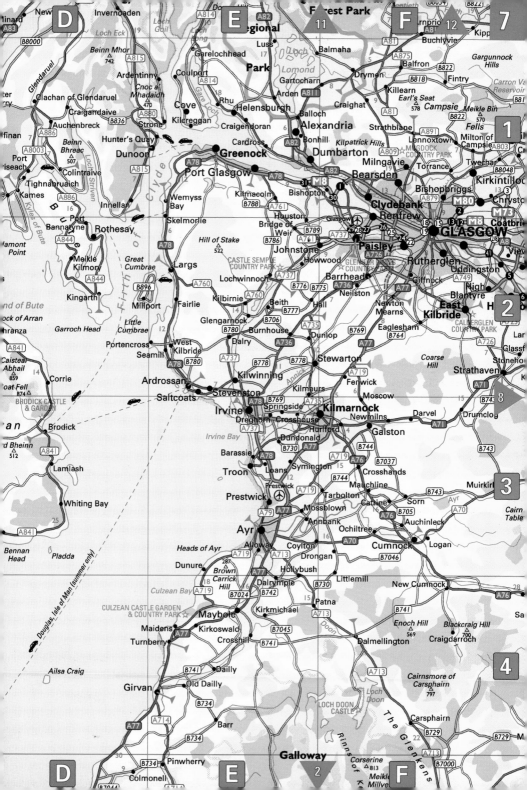

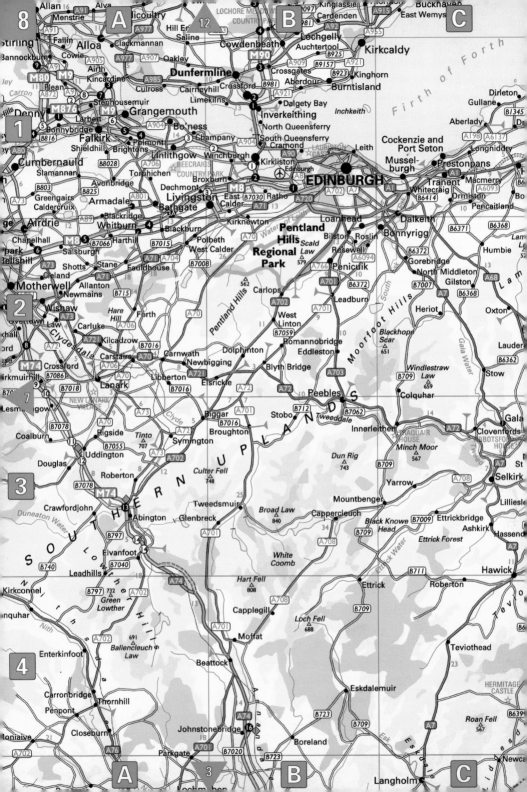

△ 14

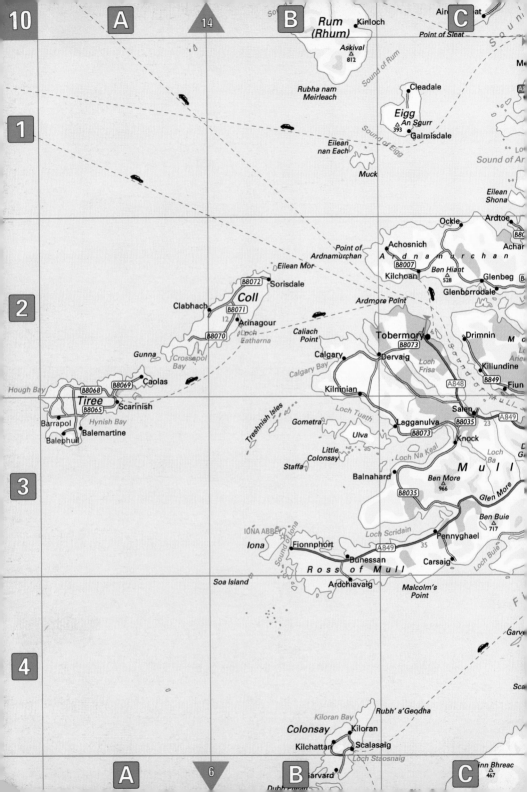

*Rum
(Rhum)*
Kinloch
Aird'....at
Point of Sleat

Askival
△ 812

*Rubha nam
Meirleach*
Cleadale

1

Eigg
An Sgurr
△ 393
Galmisdale

Sound of Rum

Sound of Eigg

*Eilean
nan Each*

Sound of Ar...
Sound of A...

Muck

*Eilean
Shona*

Ockle
Ardtoe
Achosnich
Achar
B8...

Point of
Ardnamurchan
Kilchoan
A d n a m u r c h a n
B8007
Ben Hiant
△ 528
Glenbeg
B...

Eilean Mor
Sorisdale
Glenborrodale

B8072
Coll
B8071
Clabhach
Ardmore Point

2
Arinagour
12
Tobermory
B8073
Drimnin
M...

B8070
*Loch
Eatharna*
*Caliach
Point*
Dervaig
*Loch
Frisa*
Killundine
B849
Fiun

Gunna
Calgary
Loch...
Arie...

*Crossapol
Bay*
Caolas
Calgary Bay
Kilninian
A848

Hough Bay
B8068 B8069
Scarinish
Loch Tuath
Lagganulva
B8035
A849
23

Tiree
B8065
Treshnish Isles
Gometra
B8073
Knock

Barrapol
Hynish Bay
Balemartine
Ulva
Mull
*Loch
Ba*
G...

Balephuil
*Little
Colonsay*
Loch Na Keal

Staffa
Balnahard
Ben More
△ 966

3
B8035
Glen More

Ben Buie
△ 717

IONA ABBEY
Loch Scridain
Pennyghael

Iona
Fionnphort
A849
35
Carsaig
Loch Buie

Soa Island
Bunessan
Ross of Mull

Ardchiavaig
*Malcolm's
Point*

Fi...

4
Garve...

Sca...

Kiloran Bay
Rubh' a'Geodha

Colonsay
Kiloran
Scalasaig
Kilchattan
Loch Staosnaig

▽ 6
...inn Bhreac
△ 467
...arvard
Dubh...

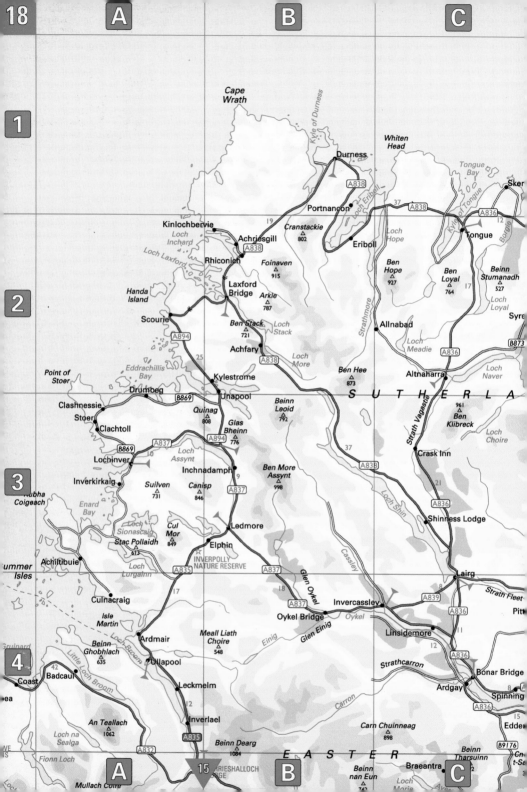

SHETLAND ISLANDS

22

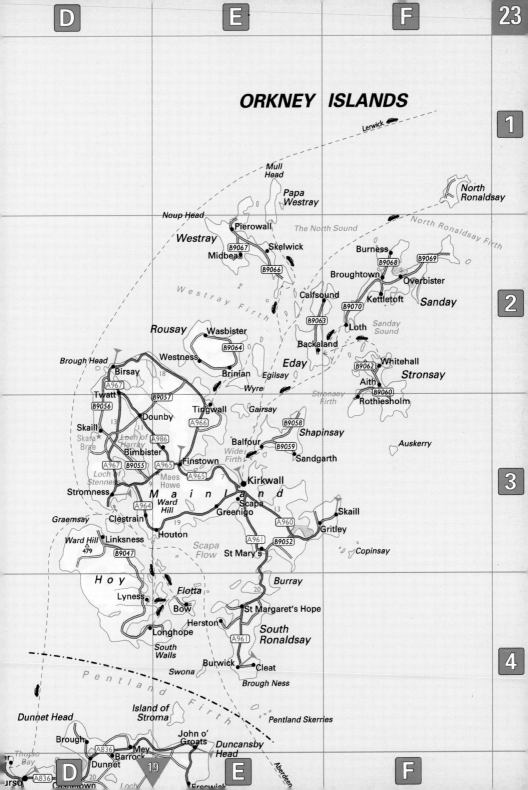

ORKNEY ISLANDS

Lerwick

Mull Head

Papa Westray

Noup Head

North Ronaldsay

Westray

Pierowall

The North Sound

North Ronaldsay Firth

B9067 Skelwick
Midbea
B9066

Burness
B9068   B9069
Broughtown
Overbister
Kettletoft
Calfsound
Sanday
B9070
B9063   Loth
Sanday Sound

Westray Firth

Rousay   Wasbister
Westness   B9064
Brinian   Egilsay
Eday   Backaland
Whitehall
B9062
Stronsay
Aith
B9060
Rothiesholm

Brough Head
Birsay   18
A967
Twatt
B9056   B9057
Dounby   13
Tingwall   Wyre
A966   Gairsay
Skaill   Loch of Harray
Skara Brae   A986
Bimbister
A967   A965   B9055   A965
Stromness   Finstown
Loch of Stenness
Maes Howe
9
Mainland   7
Ward Hill
A964
Clestrain   19
Graemsay   Houton
Ward Hill   Linkness
479   B9047
Scapa Flow

Egilsay
Wyre
Gairsay

Stronsay Firth

Balfour   Shapinsay
B9059
Sandgarth   B9058

Auskerry

Kirkwall
Scapa
Greenigo   13
A960
Skaill
Gritley
A961   B9052
St Mary's
Copinsay

Hoy
Lyness   Flotta
Bow
Longhope
Herston
South Walls
Swona
Burwick   Cleat
Brough Ness

Burray
20
St Margaret's Hope
South Ronaldsay
A961

Pentland Firth

Pentland Skerries

Dunnet Head
Island of Stroma
John o' Groats
Duncansby Head

Brough
A836   Mey
Barrock
Dunnet
20   19
Thurso Bay
A836

Aberdeen

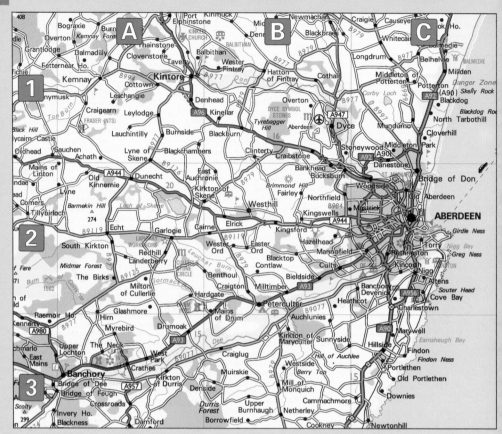

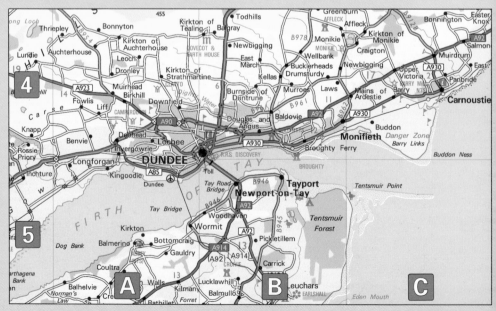

0 1 2 3 4 5 miles
0 1 2 3 4 5 6 7 8 km

D **E** **F**

Hills

Lennox Forest of Campsie
Kinkell
Cochno Edinbarpet A803 Twechar Croy Dullatur
Milngavie Baldernock A81 Dougalston Torrance Kirkintilloch Waterside Condorrat CUMBERNAULD
A810 Balmore Lenzie Moodiesburn A80 Luggie
Bearsden A879 A807 Cadder A803 Auchinloch Chryston Mollinsburn Glenboig A73 Green
Drumchapel A809 Bishopbriggs M80 Muirhead Gartcosh M73 Glenmavie Stand Wattston Calde
CLYDEBANK Maryhill Springburn A80 Stepps Woodilee A73 Riggend Rawyards
Inchinnan Yoker Partick Gartcosh COATBRIDGE A8010 AIRDRIE Chapel
Renfrew A814 Govan GLASGOW A8 Shettleston A89 Whifflet Calderbank
Glasgow M8 A89 A775 Holytown Mossend A723
PAISLEY Nitshill RUTHERGLEN Tollcross Tannochside Viewpark Bellshill Cleland
Pollokshaws A77 Carmyle Cambuslang Uddingston Bothwell
Thornliebank Castlemilk Flemington Calderglen Bothwell High New
A736 Barrhead B773 Giffnock A749 Stonefield Blantyre HAMILTON MOTHERWELL
Neilston Clarkston Carmunnock Nerston Hamilton M74
Neilston Newton Waterfoot Busby A726 Lymekilns Hillcrest Allanton W
Pad Mearns Mearns Thorntonhall EAST Hellbrae Low
Malletsheugh KILBRIDE CALDERGLEN Meikle Waters Larkhall Machan
Eaglesham Jackton Torrance Earnock Eddlewood
Ballageich Polnoon Crutherland Quarter Fairholm
Windy Hill Auldhouse Limekilnburn
Yet Rutherend

1
2
3

D **E** **F**

A823(M) Hillend A921 Barnhill Bay Inchkeith
A985 Rosyth Dalgety Inchcolm
Inverkeithing Bay St Davids St Colm's ABBEY Inchmickery
St Margaret's B980 Hope North Queensferry Forth FIRTH
HOPETOUN Forth Bridge Inch Garvie Hound Point Black Rocks
Abercorn A904 Road Bridge Toll DALMENY Cramond Island Cockenzie and
South A8000 A90 Eagle Rock Leith Port Seton
Queensferry Dalmeny A901 A199 Prestonpans
M9 Kirkliston Cramond Blackhall Portobello Musselburgh Levenhall
Newbridge A902 Edinburgh EDINBURGH Joppa Inveresk Wallyford
Burnside (Turnhouse) A8 Arthur's Seat Duddingston Newcraighall
M8 Ratho Gogar Corstorphine Niddrie A6095 Old Craighall Whitecraig
Ratho Station Morningside Craigmillar A6106 Gilmerton Crossgatehall
Hermiston A720 Blackford Libberton A720 Cousland
Wilkieston Juniper Craiglockhart Hill Danderhall Millerhill
East Green A70 Colinton A702 Gilmerton Kaimes Eskbank Dalkeith A68
Calder Currie Fairmilehead A701 Straiton Lasswade
Kirknewton Sta HILLEND SKI Loanhead Houses
Oakbank Kirknewton CENTRE Bonnyrigg

PENTLAND

4

INDEX TO PLACE NAMES

Abbreviations
Aber.   Aberdeenshire
Arg. & B.   Argyll & Bute
Bord.   Borders
C.Ab.   City of Aberdeen
Cumb.   Cumbria
D. & G.   Dumfries & Galloway
Dur.   County Durham

E.Ayr.   East Ayrshire
E.Dun.   East Dunbartonshire
E.Loth.   East Lothian
E.Renf.   East Renfrewshire
Edin.   City of Edinburgh
Glas.   City of Glasgow
High.   Highland
Midloth.   Midlothian

N.Lan.   North Lanarkshire
N.Yorks   North Yorkshire
Nhumb.   Northumberland
Ork.   Orkney
P. & K.   Perthshire & Kinross
Renf.   Renfrewshire
S.Ayr.   South Ayrshire
S.Lan.   South Lanarkshire

Shet.   Shetland
Stir.   Stirling
T. & W.   Tyne & Wear
W.Isles   Western Isles
W.Loth.   West Lothian

Abbeytown 3 E2
Aberchirder 17 D2
Aberdeen 17 F4
Aberdeen 24 C2
Aberdeen (Dyce) Airport
   17 E4
**Aberdeen (Dyce) Airport
   24 B1**
Aberdour 8 B1
Aberfeldy 12 B2
Aberfoyle 12 A4
Aberlady 8 C1
Aberlemno 13 E2
Abernethy 12 C4
Aberuthven 12 C4
Abhainnsuidhe 21 D3
Abington 8 A3
Aboyne 17 D4
Achadh Mór 21 E2
Achahoish 6 C1
Acharacle 10 C2
Achath 24 A1
Achavanich 19 E2
Achfary 18 B2
Achiltibuie 18 A3
Achintee 15 D3
Achnacroish 11 D3
Achnasheen 15 E2
Achosnich 10 C2
Achriesgill 18 B2
Acomb 4 B1
Affleck 24 B4
Aird Asaig 21 D3
Aird of Sleat 14 B4
Airdrie N.Lan. 8 A2
Airdrie N.Lan. 25 F2
Airidh a'Bhruaich 21 E2
Airth 8 A1
Aith Ork. 23 F2
Aith Shet. 22 B3
Akeld 9 E3
Alexandria 7 E1
Alford Aber. 17 D4
Allanton N.Lan. 8 A2
Allanton S.Lan. 25 F3
Allendale Town 4 B2
Allenheads 4 B2
Allnabad 18 C2
Alloa 8 A1
Allonby 3 E2
Alloway 7 E3
Alness 16 A2
Alnmouth 9 F4
Alnwick 9 F4
Alston 4 A2
Altens 24 C2
Altnafeadh 11 F2
Altnaharra 18 C2
Alva 12 B4
Alves 16 B2
Alvie 16 A4
Alyth 13 D2
Amble 9 F4
Ambleside 3 F4
Amulree 12 B3
Ancroft 9 E2
Ancrum 9 D3
Annan 3 E1
Annbank 7 E3
Annfield Plain 4 C2
Anstruther 13 E4
An t-Òb 21 D4
An Tairbeart 21 E3
Aoradh 6 A2
Appleby-in-Westmorland
   4 A3
Applecross 14 C3
Arbirlot 13 E3

Arbroath 13 E3
Ardchiavaig 10 B4
Arden 7 E1
Ardentinny 7 E1
Ardeonaig 12 A3
Ardersier 16 A2
Ardfern 11 D4
Ardgay 18 C4
Ardlui 11 F4
Ardlussa 6 B1
Ardmair 18 A4
Ardminish 6 B2
Ardmolich 11 D1
Ardrishaig 6 C1
Ardrossan 7 E3
Ardtalnaig 12 A3
Ardtoe 10 C2
Ardvasar 14 C4
Arinagour 10 B2
Arisaig 10 C1
Armadale 8 A1
Arnisdale 14 C4
Arnol 21 E1
Arnprior 12 A4
Arrochar 11 F4
Ashgill 25 F3
Ashington 5 D1
Ashkirk 8 C3
Aspatria 3 E2
Attadale 15 D3
Auchallater 12 C1
Auchenblae 13 E1
Auchenbreck 7 D1
Auchencairn 3 D2
Auchencrow 9 E2
Auchindrain 11 E4
Auchinleck 7 F3
Auchinloch 25 E1
Auchlunies 24 B3
Auchmull 13 E1
Auchnagatt 17 F3
Aucholzie 13 D1
Auchterarder 12 B4
Auchtermuchty 13 D4
Auchtertool 8 B1
Auldearn 16 B2
Auldhouse 25 E3
Aultbea 15 D1
Aultguish Inn 15 E2
Aviemore 16 B4
Avoch 16 A2
Avonbridge 8 A1
Aycliffe 5 D3
Ayr 7 E3
Aysgarth 4 C4

B

Backaland 23 E2
Badcaul 18 A4
Badenscoth 17 E3
Badlipster 19 F2
Bagh a' Chaisteil (Castlebay)
   20 A4
Baile a'Mhanaich 20 A2
Baile Ailein 21 E2
Baile Mhartainn 20 A1
Bainbridge 4 B4
Balbeggie 12 C3
Balbithan 24 A1
Balblair 16 A2
Baldernock 25 D1
Baldovie 24 B4
Balemartine 10 A3
Balephuil 10 A3
Balfour 23 E3
Balfron 7 F1

Balgown 14 B2
Balgray 13 D3
Balgray 24 B4
Balhelvie 24 A5
Balintore 16 A2
Ballachulish 11 E2
Ballantrae 2 A1
Ballater 13 D1
Ballingry 12 C4
Ballinluig 12 C2
Ballintuim 12 C2
Balloch 7 E1
Ballochroy 6 C2
Ballygrant 6 A2
Balmacara 14 C3
Balmaha 7 F1
Balmedie 17 F4
Balmedie 24 C1
Balmerino 24 A5
Balmore E.Dun. 25 E1
Balmullo 24 B5
Balnacra 15 D3
Balnahard 10 C3
Balnapaling 16 A2
Balquhidder 12 A3
Baltasound 22 C1
Balvicar 11 D4
Bamburgh 9 F3
Banchory 13 E1
Banchory 24 A3
**Banchory-Devenick
   24 C2**
Banff 17 E2
Bankfoot 12 C3
Bankhead 24 B2
Bannockburn 8 A1
Barabhas 21 E1
Barassie 7 E3
Barbaraville 16 A2
Bargrennan 2 B1
Barnard Castle 4 C3
Barr 7 E4
Barrapol 10 A3
Barrhead 7 F2
Barrhead 25 D3
Barrhill 2 B1
Barrock 19 F1
Barry 24 C4
Bathgate 8 A1
Beadnell 9 F3
Bearsden 9 F1
Bearsden 25 D1
Beattock 8 B4
Beauly 15 F3
Bedale 5 D4
Bedlington 4 C1
Beith 7 E2
Belford 9 F3
Belhelvie 24 C1
Bellingham 4 B1
Bellshill N.Lan. 7 F2
Bellshill N.Lan. 25 F3
Belmont Shet. 22 C1
Belsay 4 C1
Benthoul 24 B2
Benvie 24 A4
Bernisdale 14 B2
Berriedale 19 E3
Berwick-upon-Tweed 9 E2
Bettyhill 18 C1
Bieldside 24 B2
Biggar 8 A3
Bilbster 19 F2
Billingham 5 D3
Billy Row 4 C2
Bilston Midloth. 8 B2
Bimbister 23 D2
Birkhill 24 A4

Birsay 23 D2
Birtley T.& W. 5 D2
Bishop Auckland 4 C3
Bishopbriggs 7 F1
Bishopbriggs 25 E2
Bishopton Renf. 7 F1
Bixter 22 B3
Blackbraes 24 B1
Blackburn Aber. 17 E4
Blackburn Aber. 24 B1
Blackburn W.Loth. 8 A2
Blackchambers 24 A1
Blackdog 24 C1
Blackford 12 B4
Blackhall 25 E4
Blackhall Colliery 5 D2
Blacklunans 12 C2
Blackridge 8 A1
Blacktop 24 B2
Blackwaterfoot 6 C3
Blaich 11 E1
Blair Atholl 12 B2
Blairgowrie 12 C3
Blaydon 4 C1
Blyth Nhumb. 5 D1
Blyth Bridge 8 B2
Bo'ness 8 A1
Boath 15 F2
Boat of Garten 16 B4
Boddam Aber. 17 F3
Boddam Shet. 22 B4
Bogniebrae 17 D3
Bograxie 24 A1
Boldon 5 D2
Boltby 5 D4
Bolton E.Loth. 8 C1
Bonar Bridge 18 C4
Bonawe Quarries 11 E3
Bonchester Bridge 9 D4
Bonhill 7 E1
Bonjedward 9 D3
Bonnington 24 C4
Bonnybridge 8 A1
Bonnyrigg 8 C2
Bonnyton 24 A4
Bootle Cumb. 3 E4
Boreland 8 B4
Boreraig 14 A2
Borgh 20 A4
Borgue D.& G. 2 C2
Borgue High. 19 E3
Borrowdale 3 F3
Borrowfield 24 B3
Borve 14 B2
Bothel 3 E2
Bothwell 25 F3
Bottomcraig 24 A5
Bournmoor 5 D2
Bow 23 D3
Bowburn 5 D2
Bowes 4 B3
Bowmore 6 A2
Bowness-on-Solway 3 E1
Bowness-on-Windermere
   3 F4
Bracadale 14 A3
Braco 12 B4
Bracora 11 D1
Brae 22 B2
Braeantra 15 F1
Braemar 12 C1
Bragar 21 E1
Braithwaite 3 E3
Brampton Cumb. 4 A2
Brandon Dur. 4 C2
Breakish 14 C4
Breanais 21 D2
Breascleit 21 E2

Brechin 13 E2
Bridgend Angus 13 E2
Bridgend Moray 16 C3
Bridgend (Islay) Arg. & B.
   6 A2
Bridgend (Lochgilphead)
   Arg. & B. 6 C1
Bridge of Allan 12 B4
Bridge of Balgie 12 A2
Bridge of Cally 12 C2
Bridge of Craigisla 13 D2
Bridge of Don 17 F4
Bridge of Don 24 C2
Bridge of Dun 13 E2
Bridge of Dye 13 E1
Bridge of Earn 12 C4
Bridge of Orchy 11 F3
Bridge of Walls 22 B3
Bridge of Weir 7 E2
Brigham 3 E3
Brightons 8 A1
Brig o'Turk 12 A4
Brinian 23 E2
Broadford 14 C4
Brochel 14 B3
Brockick 7 D3
Brompton 5 D4
Brompton on Swale 4 C4
Brora 19 D4
Brotton 5 E3
Brough Cumb. 4 B3
Brough High. 19 E1
Brough Shet. 22 C2
Broughton Bord. 8 B3
Broughton in Furness 3 E4
Broughtown 23 F2
Broughty Ferry 13 E3
Broughty Ferry 24 B4
Broxburn 8 B1
Brunton 24 A5
Buchlyvie 7 F1
Buckhaven 13 D4
Buckie 17 D2
Bucklerheads 24 B4
Bucksburn 17 E4
Bucksburn 24 B2
Buddon 24 C4
Buldoo 19 E1
Bunessan 10 B3
Burgh by Sands 3 F2
Burghead 16 B2
Burness 23 F2
Burnhervie 24 A1
Burnhouse 7 E2
Burnmouth 9 E2
Burnopfield 4 C2
Burnside 24 A1
Burnside of Duntrune 24 B4
Burntisland 8 B1
Burravoe 22 C2
Burrelton 12 C3
Burwick 23 E4
Busby E.Renf. 25 D3
Buttermere 3 E3

C

Cadder 25 E1
Cairnbaan 6 C1
Cairndow 11 E4
Cairne 24 B2
Cairneyhill 8 A1
Cairnryan 2 A1
Calanais 21 E2
Caldbeck 3 F2
Calderbank 25 F2
Caldercruix 8 A1
Calderglen 25 E3

Caldwell 4 C3
Calfsound 23 E2
Calgary 10 B2
Callander 12 A4
Calvine 12 B2
Camasnacroise 11 D2
Cambuslang 25 E2
Cammachmore 24 C3
Campbeltown 6 C3
Camptown 9 D4
Cannich 15 E3
Canonbie 3 F1
Caolas 10 A2
Caolas Scalpaigh 21 E3
Cappercleuch 8 B3
Capplegill 8 B4
Caputh 12 C3
Carbost (Loch Harport) 14 B3
Carbost (Loch Snizort Beag)
 14 B3
Cardenden 13 D4
Cardross 7 E1
Cargenbridge 3 D1
Cargill 12 C3
Carlabhagh 21 E1
Carlisle 3 F2
Carlops 8 B2
Carluke 8 A2
Carmunnock 25 E3
Carmyle 25 E2
Carmyllie 13 E3
Carnbee 13 E4
Carnbo 12 C4
Carnoustie 13 E3
Carnoustie 24 C4
Carnwath 8 A2
Carradale 6 C3
Carrbridge 16 B4
Carrick 24 B5
Carronbridge 8 A4
Carsaig 10 C3
Carsluith 2 C2
Carsphairn 7 F4
Carstairs 8 A2
Castle Carrock 4 A2
Castle Douglas 3 D2
Castle Kennedy 2 A2
Castlemilk 25 E3
Castleside 4 C2
Castleton *N.Yorks.* 5 E4
Castletown *High.* 19 E1
Catrine 7 F3
Catterick 4 C4
Catterick Camp 4 C4
Causeyend 24 C1
Cawdor 16 A2
Ceann a'Bháigh 20 A1
Cearsiadar 21 E2
Ceres 13 D4
Champany 8 A1
Chapelhall 8 A2
Chapelhall 25 F2
Charlestown *C.Ab.* 17 F4
Charlestown *C.Ab.* 24 C2
Charlestown of Aberlour
 16 C3
Chatton 9 E3
Chester-le-Street 5 D2
Chesters 9 D4
Chilton 5 D3
Chirnside 9 E2
Chopwell 4 C2
Christon Bank 9 F3
Chryston 7 F1
Chryston 25 E1
Cille Bhrighde 20 A3
Clabhach 10 A2
Clachan (Kintyre) *Arg. & B.*
 6 C2
Clachan (Loch Fyne)
 Arg. & B. 11 E4
Clachan (Raasay) *High.*
 14 B3
Clachan of Glendaruel 7 D1
Clachtoll 18 A3
Clackmannan 8 A1
Cladich 11 E3
Claggan 11 D2
Claonaig 6 C2
Clarkston 25 D3

Clashmore 16 A1
Clashnessie 18 A3
Cleadale 10 C1
Cleadon 5 D1
Cleat 23 E4
Cleator Moor 3 E3
Cleland 8 A2
Cleland 25 F3
Clestrain 23 D3
Clinterty 24 B1
Closeburn 8 A4
Cloughton 5 F4
Clova 13 D1
Clovenfords 8 C3
Clovenstone 24 A1
Cloverhill 24 C1
Clovullin 11 E2
Clunes 11 E1
Clydebank 7 F1
Clydebank 25 D2
Coalburn 8 A3
Coast 15 D1
Coatbridge 7 F2
Coatbridge 25 F2
Cock Bridge 16 C4
Cockburnspath 9 D1
Cockenzie & Port Seton 8 C1
Cockermouth 3 E3
Cockfield 4 C3
Coldingham 9 E2
Coldstream 9 E3
Colintraive 7 D1
Collafirth 22 B2
Collieston 17 F3
Collin 3 E1
Colmonell 2 A1
Colnabaichin 16 C4
Colquhar 8 C2
Comrie 12 B3
Condorrat 25 F1
Coniston 3 F4
Connel 11 D3
Conon Bridge 15 F2
Consett 4 C2
Contin 15 F2
Contlaw 24 B2
Cookney 24 B3
Copley 4 C3
Corbridge 4 B1
Cornhill 17 D2
Cornhill-on-Tweed 9 E3
Corpach 11 E1
Corrie 7 D3
Corsock 3 D1
Corstorphine 25 D4
Coshieville 12 B2
Cothall 24 B1
Cottown 24 A1
Coulport 7 E1
Coultra 24 A5
Coundon 4 C3
Coupar Angus 13 D3
Cove 14 C1
Cove Bay 17 F4
Cove Bay 24 C2
Cowdenbeath 8 B1
Cowie 8 A1
Cowshill 4 B2
Coylton 7 E3
Coylumbridge 16 B4
Craibstone 24 B1
Craichie 13 E2
Craig 15 D3
Craigandaive 7 D1
Craigdarroch 7 F4
Craigearn 24 A1
Craigellachie 16 C3
Craigendoran 7 E1
Craighat 7 F1
Craigie 24 C1
Craiglockhart 25 E4
Craiglug 24 B3
Craigmillar 25 E4
Craignure 11 D3
Crail 13 E4
Cramlington 5 D1
Cramond 8 B1
Cramond 25 D4

Cranshaws 9 D2
Crask Inn 18 C3
Craster 9 F3
Crathes 24 A3
Crathie 13 D1
Crawfordjohn 8 A3
Creag Ghoraidh 20 B2
Creetown 2 C2
Creich 24 A5
Crianlarich 11 F3
Crieff 12 B3
Crimond 17 F2
Crinan 11 D4
Crocketford or Ninemile Bar
 3 D1
Cromarty 16 A2
Crook 4 C3
Crookham 9 E3
Crosbost 21 E2
Crosby Ravensworth 4 A3
Crossaig 6 C2
Crosscanonby 3 E2
Crossford *Fife* 8 B1
Crossford *S.Lan.* 8 A2
Crossgates *Fife* 8 B1
Crosshands 7 F3
Crosshill 7 E4
Crosshouse 7 E3
Crossmichael 2 C1
Crossroads 24 A3
Croy *High.* 16 A3
Croy *N.Lan.* 7 F1
Croy *N.Lan.* 25 F1
Cruden Bay 17 F3
Crulabhig 21 E2
Crutherland 25 E3
Culbokie 15 F2
Culdrain 17 D3
Cullen 17 D2
Cullicudden 16 A2
Cullipool 11 D4
Cullivoe 22 C1
Culnacraig 18 A4
Culnaknock 14 B2
Culross 8 A1
Culswick 22 B3
Cults *C.Ab.* 17 E4
Cults *C.Ab.* 24 B2
Cumberland 8 A1
Cuminestown 17 E2
Cumnock 7 F3
Cumbernauld 25 F1
Cunningsburgh 22 B4
Cupar 13 D4

D

Dacre 3 F3
Dail Bho Thuath 21 F1
Dailly 7 E4
Dairsie 13 D4
Dalabrog 20 A3
Dalbeattie 3 D2
Dalgety Bay 8 B1
Dalkeith 8 C2
Dallas 16 B2
Dalmadilly 24 A1
Dalmally 11 E3
Dalmellington 7 F4
Dalmeny 25 D4
Dalnavie 16 A2
Dalry 7 E2
Dalrymple 7 E4
Dalserf 25 F3
Dalston 3 F2
Dalwhinnie 12 A1
Danby 5 E4
Danestone 24 C1
Darlington 5 D3
Darnford 24 A3
Darra 17 E3
Darvel 7 F3
Dava 16 B3
Daviot 16 A3
Dearham 3 E3
Dechmont 8 A1
Denhead *Angus* 24 A4
Denhead *C.Ab.* 24 A1
Denholm 9 D3
Denmill 24 B1

Denny 8 A1
Denside 24 B3
Dervaig 10 C2
Diabaig 14 C2
Dingwall 15 F2
Dinnet 17 D4
Dippen 6 C3
Dirleton 8 C1
Distington 3 E3
Dochgarroch 15 F3
Doddington 9 E3
Dollar 12 B4
Dolphinton 8 B2
Dores 15 F3
Dornie 15 D3
Dornoch 16 A1
Dougalston *25 D1*
Dougarie 6 C3
Douglas *S.Lan.* 8 A3
Douglas & Angus 24 B4
Douglastown 13 D2
Dounby 23 D3
Doune 12 B4
Dounreay 19 E1
Dowally 12 C2
Downfield 24 A4
Downies 24 C3
Dreghorn 7 E3
Drem 8 C1
Drimnin 10 C2
Drongan 7 F3
Dronley 24 A4
Druimdrishaig 6 C1
Drumbeg 18 A2
Drumclog 7 F3
Drumlithie 13 F1
Drummore 2 A2
Drumnadrochit 15 F3
Drumoak 24 A3
Drumsturdy 24 B4
Drymen 7 F1
Duddingston 25 E4
Duddo 9 E2
Dufftown 16 C3
Duirinish 14 C3
Dullatur 25 F1
Dulnain Bridge 16 B3
Dumbarton 7 E1
Dumfries 3 D1
Dunbar 9 D1
Dunbeath 19 E3
Dunblane 12 B4
Dundee 13 D3
Dundee 24 B5
Dundee Airport 24 A5
Dundonald 7 E3
Dundreggan 15 E4
Dundrennan 3 D2
Dunecht 17 E4
Dunecht 24 A2
Dunfermline 8 B1
Dunkeld 12 C3
Dunlop 7 E2
Dunnet 19 E1
Dunning 12 C4
Dunoon 7 D1
Dunragit 2 A2
Dunscore 3 D1
Dunure 7 E4
Dunvegan 14 A3
Durham 5 D2
Durness 18 B1
Dyce 17 E4
Dyce 24 B1
Dyke 16 B2
Dykehead 13 D2

E

Eaglescliffe 5 D3
Eaglesfield 3 E1
Eaglesham 7 F2
Eaglesham 25 D3
Earlston 9 D3
Earsairidh 20 A4
Easdale 11 D4
Easington *Dur.* 5 D2
Easington Colliery 5 D2

East Auchronie 24 B2
East Calder 8 B1
Easter Lednathie 13 D2
Easter Ord 24 B2
Easter Quarff 22 B4
Eastgate 4 B2
East Haven 13 E3
East Haven 24 C4
East Kilbride 7 F2
East Kilbride 25 E3
East Linton 9 D1
East March 24 B4
Eastriggs 3 F1
East Wemyss 13 D4
Ecclaw 9 D1
Ecclefechan 3 E1
Eccles *Bord.* 9 D2
Echt 17 E4
Echt 24 A2
Eckford 9 D3
Edderton 16 A1
Eddleston 8 B2
Eddlewood 25 F3
Edinburgh 8 B1
Edinburgh 25 E4
Edinburgh (Turnhouse) Airport
 8 B1
**Edinburgh (Turnhouse)Airport
 25 D4**
Edlingham 9 F4
Edmundbyres 4 C2
Edzell 13 E2
Egglescliffe 5 D3
Eglingham 9 F3
Egremont 3 E3
Egton 5 F4
Einacleit 21 D2
Elgin 16 C2
Elgol 14 B4
Elie 13 E4
Ellingham 9 F3
Ellington 9 F4
Ellon 17 F3
Elphin 18 B3
Elphinstone 25 F4
Elrick 24 B2
Elsdon 9 E4
Elsrickle 8 B2
Elvanfoot 8 A3
Embleton 9 F3
Enterkinfoot 8 A4
Eoropaidh 21 F1
Eriboll 18 B2
Errogie 15 F4
Errol 13 D3
Esh Winning 4 C2
Eskdalemuir 8 B4
Eston 5 E3
Etteridge 12 A1
Ettrick 8 B4
Ettrickbridge 8 C3
Evanton 15 F2
Eyemouth 9 E2

F

Faifley 25 D1
Fairholm 25 F3
Fairley 24 B2
Fairlie 7 E2
Falkirk 8 A1
Falkland 13 D4
Fallin 8 A1
Falstone 4 A1
Farr 16 A3
Fauldhouse 8 A2
Fearnmore 14 C2
Felling 5 D1
Felton 9 F4
Fenwick *E.Ayr.* 7 F2
Fenwick *Nhumb.* 9 F2
Feochaig 6 C4
Feolin Ferry 6 B2
Fern 13 E2
Ferness 16 B3
Ferryden 13 E2
Ferryhill 5 D3
Feshiebridge 16 A4
Fettercairn 13 E1

Fetternear Ho. 24 A1
Finavon 13 E2
Findhorn 16 B2
Findochty 17 D2
Findon 24 C3
Finnygaud 17 D2
Finstown 23 E3
Fintry 7 F1
Fionnphort 10 B3
Fishburn 5 D3
Fiunary 10 C2
Flemington 25 E3
Flimby 3 E3
Flodden 9 E3
Fochabers 16 C2
Ford *Arg. & B.* 9 E3
Ford *Nhumb.* 11 D4
Fordoun 13 F1
Fordyce 17 D2
Forfar 13 D2
Forgandenny 12 C3
Forgie 16 C2
Forres 16 B2
Forsinard 19 D2
Forth 8 A2
Fortingall 12 B2
Fortrose 16 A2
Fort William 11 E1
Foulden 9 E2
Fowlis 24 A4
Foyers 15 F4
Freswick 19 F1
Freuchie 13 D4
Friockheim 13 E2
Frizington 3 E3
Funzie 22 C1
Furnace 11 E4
Fyvie 17 E3

G

Gainford 4 C3
Gairloch 14 C1
Galashiels 8 C3
Galmisdale 10 C1
Galston 7 F3
Gardenstown 17 E2
Garderhouse 22 B3
Garelochhead 7 E1
Garlieston 2 C2
Garlogie 24 A2
Garsdale Head 4 B4
Gartcosh 25 E2
Gartocharn 7 E1
Garvald 9 D1
Garvamore 12 A1
Garvard 6 A1
Garve 15 F2
Gatehouse of Fleet 2 C2
Gateshead 5 D2
Gauldry 24 A5
Gawthrop 4 A4
Gearraidh na h-Aibhne 21 E2
Giffnock 7 F2
Giffnock 25 D3
Gifford 8 C1
Gillamoor 5 E4
Gilling West 4 C4
Gilmerton 12 B3
Gilsland 4 A1
Gilston 8 C2
Girlsta 22 B3
Girvan 7 E4
Glamis 13 D2
Glanton 9 E3
Glasgow 7 F2
Glasgow 25 D2
Glasgow Airport 7 F2
Glashmore 24 A2
Glassford 7 F2
Glenbarr 6 B3
Glenbeg 10 C2
Glenboig 25 F2
Glenborrodale 10 C2
Glenbreck 8 B3
Glenbrittle 14 B4
Glencaple 3 E1
Glencarse 12 C3
Glencoe 11 E2

Gleneagles 12 B4
Glenegedale 6 A2
Glenelg 14 C4
Glenfarg 12 C4
Glenfinnan 11 D1
Glengarnock 7 E2
Glenkindie 17 D4
Glenluce 2 A2
Glenmavis 25 F2
Glenrothes 13 D4
Gogar 25 D4
Golspie 19 D4
Gordon 9 D2
Gorebridge 8 C2
Gosforth *Cumb.* 3 E4
Gosforth *T. & W.* 4 C1
Gourdon 13 F2
Grabhair 21 E2
Grandtully 12 B2
Grangemouth 8 A1
Grantlodge 24 A1
Grantown-on-Spey 16 B3
Grantshouse 9 D2
Grasmere 3 F4
Grayrigg 4 A4
Great Ayton 5 E3
Great Broughton 5 E4
Great Clifton 3 E3
Great Salkeld 4 A2
Greenburn 24 B4
Greengairs 8 A1
Greengairs 25 F1
Greenhead 4 A1
Greenigo 23 E3
Greenlaw 9 D2
Greenloaning 12 B4
Greenock 7 E1
Gretna 3 F1
Greystoke 3 F3
Griais 21 F1
Gritley 23 E3
Grizebeck 3 E4
Guide Post 4 C1
Guildtown 12 C3
Guisborough 5 E3
Gullane 8 C1
Gutcher 22 C1

H

Hackness 5 F4
Haddington 8 C1
Halkirk 19 E2
Hall 7 E2
Haltwhistle 4 A1
Ham *Shet.* 22 A3
Hamilton 7 F2
Hamilton 25 F3
Hamnavoe (Mainland) *Shet.*
22 B4
Hamnavoe (Yell) *Shet.* 22 C2
Hardgate 24 A2
Haroldswick 22 C1
Harrietfield 12 C3
Harthill *N.Lan.* 8 A2
Hartlepool 5 E3
Hassendean 8 C3
Haswell 5 D2
Hatton *Aber.* 17 F3
Hatton of Fintray 24 B1
Haugh of Urr 3 D1
Hawes 4 B4
Hawick 8 C3
Hawkshead 3 F4
Haydon Bridge 4 B1
Hazelhead 24 B2
Hazelton Walls 24 A5
Healeyfield 4 C2
Heathcot 24 B2
Hebburn 5 D1
Heglibister 22 B3
Helensburgh 7 E1
Helmsdale 19 E3
Helmsley 5 E4
Heriot 8 C2
Hermiston 25 D4
Herston 23 E4
Hetton-le-Hole 5 D2
Hexham 4 B1

High Blantyre 7 F2
High Blantyre 25 E3
High Etherley 4 C3
High Hawsker 5 F4
High Hesket 3 F2
High Lorton 3 E3
Hill End 12 C4
Hill of Fearn 16 A1
Hillside *Aber.* 24 C3
Hillside *Angus* 13 E2
Hillside *Shet.* 22 B2
Hillswick 22 B2
Hinderwell 5 F3
Hirn 24 A2
Hollybush *E.Ayr.* 7 E4
Holytown 25 F2
Holywood 3 D1
Hopeman 16 B2
Horden 5 D2
Houbie 22 C1
Houghton le Spring 5 D2
Houndslow 9 D2
Houston 7 E2
Houton 23 E3
Howwood 7 E2
Huisinis 21 D3
Humbie 8 C2
Hunter's Quay 7 E1
Huntly 17 D3
Hurlford 7 F3
Hurworth-on-Tees 5 D3
Hutton Rudby 5 D4

I

Idrigil 14 B2
Inchbare 13 E2
Inchnadamph 18 B3
Inchture 13 D3
Ingleton *Dur.* 4 C3
Innellan 7 D2
Innerleithen 8 C3
Insch 17 D3
Inveralligan 14 C2
Inverallochy 17 F2
Inverarity 13 D3
Inverarnan 11 F4
Inverbervie 13 F1
Invercassley 18 C4
Invercharnan 11 E2
Inveresk 25 F4
Inverey 12 C1
Invergarry 15 E4
Invergordon 16 A2
Invergowrie 24 A4
Inverinan 11 E4
Inverkeilor 13 E2
Inverkeithing 8 B1
Inverkirkaig 18 A3
Inverlael 15 E1
Invermoriston 15 F4
Inverness 16 A3
Inverness (Dalcross) Airport
16 A2
Invernoaden 11 E4
Inverurie 17 E4
Irvine 7 E3
Isbister (Mainland) *Shet.*
22 B1
Isbister (Whalsay) *Shet.*
22 C2
Isle of Whithorn 2 C2

J

Jackton 25 D3
Jarrow 5 D1
Jedburgh 9 D3
Jemimaville 16 A2
John o' Groats 19 F1
Johnstone 7 E2
Johnstonebridge 8 B4
Joppa *Edin.* 25 F4

K

Kames 7 D1
Keillmore 6 C1
Keiss 19 F1
Keith 17 D2

Kellas *Angus* 13 D3
Kellas *Angus* 24 B4
Kellas *Moray* 16 C2
Kelso 9 D3
Kelty 12 C4
Kemnay 17 E4
Kemnay 24 A1
Kendal 4 A4
Kenmore 12 B2
Kennacraig 6 C2
Kennethmont 17 D3
Kennoway 13 D4
Kensaleyre 14 B2
Kentallen 11 E2
Keswick 3 F3
Kettletoft 23 F2
Kielder 9 D4
Kilberry 6 C2
Kilbirnie 7 E2
Kilcadzow 8 A2
Kilchattan 6 A1
Kilchattan 10 B4
Kilchenzie 6 C3
Kilchiaran 6 A2
Kilchoan 10 C2
Kilchoman 6 A2
Kilchrenan 11 E3
Kilconquhar 13 E4
Kilcreggan 7 E1
Kildonan Lodge 19 D3
Kilfinan 7 D1
Kilham *Nhumb.* 9 E3
Killean 6 C2
Killearn 7 F1
Killichonan 12 A2
Killiecrankie 12 B2
Killin 12 A3
Killingworth 5 D1
Killundine 10 C2
Kilmacolm 7 E1
Kilmalieu 11 D2
Kilmaluag 14 B2
Kilmany 24 A5
Kilmarnock 7 F3
Kilmartin 11 D4
Kilmaurs 7 E3
Kilmelford 11 D4
Kilmory *Arg. & B.* 6 C1
Kilmory (Rum) *High.* 14 A4
Kilninian 10 B2
Kilninver 11 D3
Kiloran 10 B4
Kilrenny 13 E4
Kilsyth 7 F1
Kilwinning 7 E2
Kinbrace 19 D3
Kincardine 8 A1
Kincardine O'Neil 17 D4
Kincorth 24 C2
Kincraig 16 A4
Kinellar 24 B1
Kingarth 7 D2
Kinghorn 8 B1
Kinglassie 13 D4
Kingoodie 24 A5
Kingsbarns 13 E4
Kingsford 24 B2
Kingshouse 12 A3
Kingston 16 C2
Kingswells 24 B2
Kingussie 16 A4
Kinkell 25 E1
Kinloch 14 B4
Kinlochard 12 A4
Kinlochbervie 18 B2
Kinlochewe 15 D2
Kinloch Hourn 15 D4
Kinlochleven 11 E2
Kinloch Rannoch 12 A2
Kinloss 16 B2
Kinmuck 24 B1
Kinross 12 C4
Kintore 17 E4
Kintore 24 A1
Kintour 6 B2
Kintra 6 A2
Kippen 12 A4
Kirkbean 3 D2
Kirkbride 3 E2

Kirkbymoorside 5 E4
Kirkby Stephen 4 B4
Kirkcaldy 8 B1
Kirkcolm 2 A1
Kirkconnel 8 A4
Kirkcowan 2 B2
Kirkcudbright 2 C2
Kirkinner 2 B2
Kirkintilloch 7 F1
Kirkintilloch 25 E1
Kirkliston 8 B1
Kirkliston 25 D4
Kirkmichael *P. & K.* 12 C2
Kirkmichael *S.Ayr.* 7 E4
Kirkmuirhill 8 A2
Kirknewton *Nhumb.* 9 E3
Kirknewton *W.Loth.* 8 B2
Kirkoswald *Cumb.* 4 A2
Kirkoswald *S.Ayr.* 7 E4
Kirkton *Fife* 24 A5
Kirkton *Arg. & B.* 11 D4
Kirkton of Auchterhouse
24 A4
Kirkton of Culsalmond 17 D3
Kirkton of Durris 13 F1
Kirkton of Durris 24 A3
Kirkton of Glenisla 13 D2
Kirkton of Kingoldrum 13 D2
Kirkton of Maryculter 24 B3
Kirkton of Menmuir 13 E2
Kirkton of Monikie 24 C4
Kirkton of Skene 17 E4
Kirkton of Skene 24 B2
Kirkton of Strathmartine
24 A4
Kirkton of Tealing 24 B4
Kirktown of Auchterless
17 E3
Kirktown of Deskford 17 D2
Kirkwall 23 E3
Kirk Yetholm 9 E3
Kirriemuir 13 D2
Knayton 5 D4
Knock 10 C3
Knockandhu 16 C4
Knockban 15 E2
Kyleakin 14 C3
Kyle of Lochalsh 14 C3
Kylerhea 14 C4
Kylestrome 18 B2

L

Ladybank 13 D4
Ladykirk 9 E2
Ladysford 17 E2
Lagg 7 D3
Laggan (Invergarry) *High.*
11 F1
Laggan (Newtonmore) *High.*
12 A1
Lagganulva 10 C3
Laide 15 D1
Lairg 18 C4
Lamlash 7 D3
Lanark 8 A2
Lanchester 4 C2
Landerberry 24 A2
Langholm 3 F1
Langwathby 4 A2
Larbert 8 A1
Largoward 13 D4
Largs 7 E2
Larkhall 8 A2
Larkhall 25 F3
Latheron 19 E2
Latheronwheel 19 E2
Lauchintilly 24 A1
Lauder 8 C2
Laurencekirk 13 E2
Laurieston 2 C1
Law 8 A2
Lawers 12 A3
Laws 24 B4
Laxford Bridge 18 B2
Laxo 22 B2
Lazonby 4 A2
Leadburn 8 B2

Leadgate 4 C2
Leadhills 8 A3
Leckmelm 15 E1
Ledaig 11 D3
Ledmore 18 B3
Leeming 5 D4
Leith 8 B1
Leith 25 E4
Lennoxtown 7 F1
Lenzie 25 E1
Leoch 24 A4
Lerwick 22 B3
Lesbury 9 F4
Leschangie 24 A1
Leslie 13 D4
Lesmahagow 8 A3
Leswalt 2 A1
Leuchars 13 D3
Leuchars 24 B5
Leumrabhagh 21 E3
Leven *Fife* 13 D4
Levenhall 25 F4
Levenwick 22 B4
Leyburn 4 C4
Leylodge 24 A1
Lhanbryde 16 C2
Libberton 8 A2
Liff 24 A4
Lilliesleaf 8 C3
Limekilnburn 25 F3
Limekilns 8 B1
Lindores 13 D4
Linlithgow 8 A1
Linsidemore 15 F1
Littlemill *E.Ayr.* 7 F4
Littlemill *High.* 16 B2
Livingston 8 B1
Loanhead 8 B2
Loans 7 E3
Lochailort 11 D1
Lochaline 10 C3
Lochans 2 A2
Locharbriggs 3 E1
Lochawe 11 E3
Loch Baghasdail
  (Lochboisdale) 20 B3
Lochcarron 15 D3
Lochdon 11 D3
Lochearnhead 12 A3
Lochee 24 A4
Lochend 15 F3
Lochgelly 12 C4
Lochgilphead 6 C1
Lochgoilhead 11 F4
Lochinver 18 A3
Lochmaben 3 E1
Loch na Madadh
  (Lochmaddy) 20 B1
Lochranza 7 D2
Loch Sgioport 20 B2
Lochwinnoch 7 E2
Lockerbie 3 E1
Lockton 5 F4
Logan 7 F3
Longbenton 5 D1
Longdrum 24 C1
Longforgan 13 D3
Longforgan 24 A5
Longframlington 9 F4
Longhope *Ork.* 23 D4
Longhorsley 9 F4
Longhoughton 9 F3
Longmanhill 17 E2
Longmorn 16 C2
Longniddry 8 C1
Longside 17 F3
Longtown 3 F1
Lossiemouth 16 C2
Loth 23 F2
Lothmore 19 E3
Lower Killeyan 6 A3
Loweswater 3 E3
Lowick 9 E3
Low Waters 25 F3
Lucklawhill 24 B5
Ludag 20 A3
Luggiebank 25 F1
Luib 14 B3
Lumphanan 17 D4
Luncarty 12 C3
Lundin Links 13 D4
Luss 7 E1
Lusta 14 A2
Lybster 19 F2
Lymekilns 25 E3
Lyne 24 A2
Lynemore 16 B3
Lynemouth 9 F4
Lyne of Skene 17 E4
Lyne of Skene 24 A1
Lyness 23 D4

M

Macduff 17 E2
Machan 25 F3
Macharioch 6 B3
Machrihanish 6 B3
Macmerry 8 C1
Maidens 7 E4
Mains of Ardestie 24 C4
Mains of Drum 24 B2
Mains of Linton 24 A2
Malletsheugh 25 D3
Mannofield 24 C2
Markinch 13 D4
Marske-by-the-Sea 5 E3
Marybank 15 F2
Maryhill *Glas.* 25 D2
Marykirk 13 E2
Marypark 16 C3
Maryport 3 E2
Marywell (near Aboyne)
  Aber. 13 E1
**Marywell (near Portlethen)
  Aber. 24 C3**
Mastrick 24 B2
Mauchline 7 F3
Maud 17 F3
Maybole 7 E4
Mealsgate 3 E2
Mearns 25 D3
Meigle 13 D3
Meikle Earnock 25 F3
Meikle Kilmory 7 D2
Meikleour 12 C3
Melby 22 A3
Melmerby 4 A2
Melrose 8 C3
Melsonby 4 C4
Melvaig 14 C1
Melvich 19 D1
Memsie 17 F2
Menstrie 12 B4
Methlick 17 E3
Methven 12 C3
Mey 19 F1
Miabhig 21 D2
Mickleton *Dur.* 4 B3
Mid Ardlaw 17 F2
Midbea 23 E2
Middleham 4 C4
Middlesbrough 5 D3
Middleton 24 B1
Middleton-in-Teesdale 4 B3
Middleton of Potterton 24 C1
Middleton Park 24 C1
Midlem 8 C3
Mid Yell 22 C1
Milfield 9 E3
Millden 24 C1
Millhouse 7 D1
Mill of Monquich 24 B3
Millport 7 D2
Milltimber 24 B2
Milltown 17 D4
Milltown of Rothiemay 17 D3
Milnathort 12 C4
Milngavie 7 F1
Milngavie 25 D1
Milovaig 14 A2
Milton *High.* 16 B2
Milton *P.& K.* 12 B3
Milton of Campsie 7 F1
Milton of Campsie 25 E1
Milton of Cullerlie 24 A2
Minard 11 E4
Minnigaff 2 B1
Mintlaw 17 F3
Moffat 8 B4
Mollinsburn 25 F1
Moniaive 8 A4
Monifieth 13 E3
Monifieth 24 B4
Monikie 24 B4
Monimail 13 D4
Monreith 2 B2
Montrose 13 E2
Moodiesburn 25 E1
Morar 10 C1
Morebattle 9 D3
Morenish 12 A3
Moresby 3 E3
Morningside *Edin.* 25 E4
Morpeth 4 C1
Moscow 7 F3
Mossat 17 D4
Mossblown 7 E3
Mosstodloch 16 C2
Motherwell 8 A2
Motherwell 25 F3
Mountbenger 8 C3
Mowtie 13 F1
Moy 16 A3
Muchalls 13 F1
Muirdrum 13 E3
Muirdrum 24 C4
Muirhead *Angus* 13 D3
Muirhead *Angus* 24 A4
Muirhead *N.Lan.* 25 E2
Muirkirk 7 F3
Muir of Fowlis 17 D4
Muir of Ord 15 F2
Muirskie 24 B3
Mulben 16 C2
Mundurno 24 C1
Munlochy 16 A2
Murroes 24 B4
Murton 5 D2
Musselburgh 8 C1
Musselburgh 25 F4
Muthill 12 B4
Mybster 19 E2
Myrebird 24 A3

N

Nairn 16 A2
Nateby 4 B4
Near Sawrey 3 F4
Neilston 7 F2
Nenthall 4 B2
Nenthead 4 B2
Nerston 25 E3
Netherley 13 F1
Netherley 24 B3
Netherton *Numb.* 9 E4
Nethy Bridge 16 B4
New Abbey 3 D1
New Aberdour 17 E2
Newarthill 25 F3
Newbiggin-by-the-Sea 5 D1
Newbigging *S.Lan.* 8 A2
**Newbigging (East) *Angus*
  24 B4**
**Newbigging (West) *Angus*
  24 B4**
Newbridge *Edin.* 25 D4
Newburgh *Aber.* 17 F3
Newburgh *Fife* 13 D4
Newburn 4 C1
Newby Bridge 3 F4
New Byth 17 F2
Newcastle (Woolsington)
  Airport 4 C1
Newcastleton 3 F1
Newcastle upon Tyne 4 C1
Newcraighall 25 F4
New Cumnock 7 F4
New Deer 17 E3
New Galloway 2 C1
Newhouse 25 F2
New Leeds 17 F2
New Luce 2 A1
Newmachar 17 E4
Newmachar 24 B1
Newmains 8 A2
Newmarket *W.Isles* 21 F2
Newmill 17 D2
Newmilns 7 F3
New Pitsligo 17 E2
Newport *High.* 19 E3
Newport-on-Tay 13 D3
Newport-on-Tay 24 B5
New Scone 12 C3
Newton *Arg. & B.* 11 E4
Newtonhill 13 F1
Newtonhill 24 C3
Newton Mearns 7 F2
Newton Mearns 25 D3
Newtonmore 16 A4
Newton Stewart 2 B1
Newtown St. Boswells 9 D3
Newtyle 13 D3
Niddrie 25 E4
Nigg 24 C2
Nisbet 9 D3
Nitshill 25 D2
Norham 9 E3
Northallerton 5 D4
North Ballachulish 11 E2
North Berwick 8 C1
North Cowton 5 D4
Northfield 24 B2
North Kessock 16 A3
North Middleton 8 C2
North Queensferry 8 B1
North Shields 5 D1
North Sunderland 9 F3
North Tarbothill 24 C1
Norwich 22 C1

O

Oakley *Fife* 8 A1
Oban 11 D3
Ochiltree 7 F3
Ockle 10 C2
Oddsta 22 C1
Old Aberdeen 24 C2
Old Craighall 25 F4
Old Dailly 7 E4
Old Kinnernie 24 A2
Oldmeldrum 17 E3
Old Portlethen 24 C3
Olgrinmore 19 E2
Ollaberry 22 B2
Onich 11 E2
Ormiston 8 C1
Orrok Ho. 24 C1
Orton 4 A4
Oskaig 14 B3
Otterburn 9 E4
Otter Ferry 7 D1
Otterswick 22 C2
Overbister 23 F2
Overton *Aber.* 24 A1
Overton *C.Ab.* 24 A2
Overtown 8 A2
Oxnam 9 D3
Oxton *Bord.* 8 C2
Oykel Bridge 15 F1

P

Paisley 7 F2
Palnackie 3 D2
Panbride 24 C4
Parton 3 D3
Partick 25 D2
Path of Condie 12 C4
Patna 7 E4
Patterdale 3 F3
Paxton 9 E2
Peebles 8 B2
Pegswood 4 C1
Peinchorran 14 B3
Pencaitland 8 C1
Penicuik 8 B2
Peninver 6 C3
Pennyghael 10 C3
Penpont 8 A4
Penrith 4 A3
Perth 12 C3
Peterculter 17 E4
Peterculter 24 B2
Peterhead 17 F3
Peterlee 5 D2
Pickering 5 F4
Pickletillem 24 B5
Pierowall 23 E2
Pinwherry 2 A1
Pirnmill 6 C2
Pitagowan 12 B2
Pitlochry 12 B2
Pitmedden 17 E3
Pitscottie 13 D4
Pittentrail 16 A1
Pittenweem 13 E4
Plains 25 F2
Plean 8 A1
Polbeth 8 A2
Polloch 11 D2
Pollokshaws 25 D2
Polmont 8 A1
Polnoon 25 D3
Polwarth 9 D2
Ponteland 4 C1
Poolewe 14 C1
Pooley Bridge 3 F3
Pool of Muckhart 12 C4
Port Appin 11 D3
Port Askaig 6 B1
Port Bannatyne 7 D2
Port Driseach 7 D1
Port Ellen 6 A2
Port Elphinstone 24 A1
Portencross 7 D2
Port Glasgow 7 E1
Port Henderson 14 C2
Portknockie 17 D2
Portlethen 13 F1
Portlethen 24 C3
Port Logan 2 A2
Portmahomack 16 B1
Portnacroish 11 D2
Portnahaven 6 A2
Portnalong 14 A3
Port nan Giúran 21 F2
Port nan Long 20 B1
Portobello 25 F4
Port of Menteith 12 A4
Portpatrick 2 A1
Portree 14 B3
Portsoy 17 D2
Port William 2 B2
Potterton 24 C1
Powburn 9 F3
Powmill 12 C4
Preston *Bord.* 9 D2
Prestonpans 8 C1
Prestonpans 25 F4
Prestwick 7 E3
Prestwick Airport 7 E3
Prudhoe 4 C2

Q

Quarter 25 F3

R

Rafford 16 B2
Rait 13 D3
Rathillet 13 D4
Rathillet 24 A5
Ratho 8 B1
Ratho 25 D4
Ratho Station 25 D4
Rattray 12 C3
Ravenglass 3 E4
Rawyards 25 F2
Reay 19 D1
Redcar 5 E3
Redcastle 15 F3
Redford 13 E3
Redhill 24 A2
Redpoint 14 C2
Reiss 19 F2
Renfrew 7 F2
Renfrew 25 D2
Rennington 9 F3
Rescobie 13 E2
Reston 9 E2
Rhiconich 18 B2
Rhu 7 E1

Rhynie 17 D3
Richmond 4 C4
Riding Mill 4 C2
Riggend 25 F2
Rigside 8 A3
Ringford 2 C2
Roadside 19 E1
Roadside of Kinneff 13 F1
Roberton *Bord.* 8 C4
Roberton *S.Lan.* 8 A3
Robin Hood's Bay 5 F4
Rochester *Nhumb.* 9 E4
Rockcliffe 3 D2
Rogart 19 D4
Roghadal 21 D4
Romanby 5 D4
Romannobridge 8 B2
Rosedale Abbey 5 E4
Rosehearty 17 F2
Rosemarkie 16 A2
Rosewell 8 B2
Roshven 11 D1
Roskhill 14 A3
Roslin 8 B2
Rothbury 9 E4
Rothes 16 C3
Rothesay 7 D2
Rothiesholm 23 F3
Rowlands Gill 4 C2
Roybridge 11 F1
Rutherend 25 E3
Rutherglen 7 F2
Rutherglen 25 E2
Ruthrieston 24 C2

S

Sacriston 4 C2
Saddell 6 C3
Saighdinis 20 B1
Salen *Arg. & B.* 10 C3
Salen *High.* 11 D2
Saline 8 A1
Salmond's Muir 24 C4
Salsburgh 8 A2
Saltburn-by-the-Sea 5 E3
Saltcoats 7 E3
Sanaigmore 6 A1
Sandgarth 23 E3
Sandhead 2 A2
Sandness 22 A3
Sandsend 5 F3
Sandwick 22 B4
Sanquhar 8 A4
Satley 4 C2
Scalasaig 10 B4
Scalby 5 F4
Scalloway 22 B3
Scapa 23 E3
Scarinish 10 A3
Sconser 14 B3
Scorton 4 C4
Scotch Corner 4 C4
Scotton 4 C4
Scourie 18 A2
Scousburgh 22 B4
Scrabster 19 E1
Scremerston 9 E2
Seaham 5 D2
Seahouses 9 F3
Seamill 7 E2
Seascale 3 E4
Seaton *Cumb.* 3 E3
Seaton Delaval 5 D1
Seaton Sluice 5 D1
Sedbergh 4 A4
Sedgefield 5 D3
Seghill 5 D1
Selkirk 8 C3
Sellafield 3 E4
Sellafirth 22 C1
Setter 22 B3
Sgiogarstaigh 21 F1
Shap 4 A3
Sherburn 5 D2
Shettleston 25 E2
Shiel Bridge 15 D4
Shieldaig 14 C2
Shieldhill 8 A1
Shilbottle 9 F4

Shildon 4 C3
Shinness Lodge 18 C3
Shiremoor 5 D1
Shotts 8 A2
Siabost 21 E1
Silloth 3 E2
Siulaisiadar 21 F2
Skaill (East Coast) *Ork.* 23 F3
Skaill (West Coast) *Ork.* 23 D3
Skaw 22 C2
Skelmorlie 7 E2
Skelton 5 E3
Skelwick 23 E2
Skerray 18 C1
Skipness 6 C2
Slamannan 8 A1
Sleights 5 F4
Sligachan 14 B3
Smailholm 9 D3
Solas 20 B1
Sorbie 2 B2
Sorisdale 10 B2
Sorn 7 F3
South Bank 5 E3
Southdean 9 D4
Southend *Arg. & B.* 6 C4
South Hetton 5 D2
South Kirkton 24 A2
South Queensferry 8 B1
South Queensferry 25 D4
South Shields 5 D1
Spean Bridge 11 F1
Spennymoor 5 D3
Spey Bay 16 C2
Spinningdale 16 A1
Spittal 19 E2
Spittal of Glenshee 12 C2
Springburn 25 E2
Springholm 3 D1
Springside 7 E3
St. Abbs 9 E1
St. Andrews 13 E4
St. Bees 3 D3
St. Combs 17 F2
St. Cyrus 13 F2
St. Fergus 17 F2
St. Fillans 12 A4
St. John's Chapel 4 B2
St. John's Town of Dalry 2 C1
St. Margaret's Hope 23 E4
St. Mary's 23 E3
St. Monans 13 E4
Stadhlaigearraidh 20 A2
Staffin 14 B2
Staindrop 4 C3
Staintondale 5 F4
Stalling Busk 4 B4
Stamfordham 4 C1
Stand 25 F2
Stane 8 A2
Stanhope 4 B2
Stanley *Dur.* 4 C2
Stanley *P. & K.* 12 C3
Stannington *Nhumb.* 4 C1
Startforth 4 C3
Stenhousemuir 8 A1
Stenness 22 A2
Stenton 9 D1
Stepps 25 E2
Stevenston 7 E3
Stewarton 7 E3
Stichill 9 D3
Stirling 8 A1
Stobo 8 B3
Stocksfield 4 C2
Stockton-on-Tees 5 D3
Stoer 18 A3
Stokesley 5 E4
Stonefield *S.Lan.* 25 E3
Stonehaven 13 F1
Stonehouse *S.Lan.* 8 A2
Stoneykirk 2 A2
Stoneywood 24 B1
Stornoway 21 F2
Stow 8 C2
Strachan 13 E1
Strachur 11 E4
Straloch 12 C2
Stranraer 2 A2

Strathaven 7 F2
Strathblane 7 F1
Strathdon 16 C4
Strathmiglo 12 C4
Strathpeffer 15 F2
Strathy 19 D1
Strathyre 12 A4
Strichen 17 F2
Stromeferry 14 C3
Stromness 23 D3
Stronachlachar 11 F4
Strone 7 E1
Strontian 11 D2
Stuartfield 17 F3
Sunderland 5 D2
Sunnyside 24 B3
Swinton *Bord.* 9 E2
Symbister 22 C3
Symington *S.Ayr.* 7 E3
Symington *S.Lan.* 8 A3
Syre 18 C2

T

Tabost 21 F1
Tain 16 A1
Talisker 14 A3
Talladale 15 D2
Tannadice 13 E2
Tannochside 25 F2
Taobh Tuath 21 D3
Tarbert (Jura) *Arg. & B.* 6 B1
Tarbert (Kintyre) *Arg. & B.* 6 C2
Tarbet 11 E4
Tarbolton 7 F3
Tarfside 13 E1
Tarrel 16 B1
Tarves 17 E3
Tavelty 24 A1
Tayinloan 6 C2
Taynuilt 11 E3
Tayport 13 D3
Tayport 24 C4
Tayvallich 6 C1
Teangue 14 C4
Tebay 4 A4
Tees-side Airport 5 D3
Temple Sowerby 4 A3
Teviothead 8 C4
Thainstone 24 A1
The Birks 24 A2
The Neuk 24 A3
Thornaby-on-Tees 5 D3
Thornhill *D. & G.* 8 A4
Thornhill *Stir.* 12 A4
Thornley 5 D2
Thornliebank 25 D3
Thornton *Fife* 13 D4
Thorntonhall 25 D3
Threlkeld 3 F3
Thriepley 24 A4
Thropton 9 E4
Thrumster 19 F2
Thursby 3 F2
Thurso 19 E1
Thwaite 4 B4
Tibbermore 12 C3
Tighnabruaich 7 D1
Tillicoultry 12 B4
Tillyfourie 17 D4
Timsgearraidh 21 D2
Tingwall 23 E3
Toab 22 B4
Tobermory 10 C2
Toberonochy 11 D4
Todhills 24 B4
Toft 22 B2
Togston 9 F4
Tolastadh a'Chaolais 21 E2
Tolastadh Úr 21 F1
Tollcross 25 E2
Toll of Birness 17 F3
Tomatin 16 A3
Tomich 16 A2
Tomintoul 16 C4
Tomnavoulin 16 C3
Tongland 2 C2
Tongue 18 C2
Tore 15 F2

Tormore 6 C3
Torphichen 8 A1
Torphins 17 D4
Torrance *E.Dun.* 7 F1
Torrance *E.Dun.* 25 E1
Torrance *S.Lan.* 25 E3
Torridon 15 D2
Torrin 14 B4
Torry 24 C2
Torthorwald 3 E1
Torver 3 F4
Toscaig 14 C3
Tow Law 4 C2
Townhead of Greenlaw 3 D1
Tranent 8 C1
Tressait 12 B2
Trimdon 5 D3
Trinity 13 E2
Trochry 12 C3
Troon 7 E3
Troutbeck 3 F4
Troutbeck Bridge 3 F4
Tummel Bridge 12 B2
Tunga 21 F2
Turnberry 7 E4
Turriff 17 E2
Twatt 23 E2
Twechar 7 F1
Twechar 25 E1
Tweedmouth 9 E2
Tweedsmuir 8 B3
Twynholm 2 C2
Tyndrum 11 F3
Tynemouth 5 D1

U

Uachdar 20 B2
Uddingston 7 F2
Uddingston 25 E2
Uddington 8 A3
Uig 14 B2
Ulbster 19 F2
Ulgham 9 F4
Ullapool 15 D1
Ulpha 3 E4
Ulsta 22 B2
Unapool 18 B2
Upper Burnhaugh 24 B3
Upper Camster 19 F2
Upper Knockando 16 C3
Upper Victoria 24 C4
Urafirth 22 B2
Ushaw Moor 4 C2
Uyeasound 22 C1

V

Valsgarth 22 C1
Veensgarth 22 B3
Vidlin 22 C2
Viewpark 7 F2
Viewpark 25 F2
Voe 22 B2

W

Walls 22 B3
Wallsend 5 D1
Wallyford 25 F4
Warcop 4 A3
Wark 4 B1
Warkworth 9 F4
Warwick Bridge 3 F2
Wasbister 23 E2
Washington *T. & W.* 5 D2
Watchgate 4 A4
Waterbeck 3 F1
Waterfoot *E.Renf.* 25 D3
Waterside *E.Dun.* 25 E1
Watten 19 F2
Wattston 25 F2
Weem 12 B2
Wellbank 24 B4
Wemyss Bay 7 E1
Wensley 4 C4
West Auckland 4 C3
West Calder 8 A2
Westerdale 19 E2
Wester Fintray 24 B1

Wester Ord 24 B2
Wester Parkgate 3 E1
Westerton 24 A3
Westgate 4 B2
Westhill *Aber.* 17 E4
Westhill *Aber.* 24 B2
West Kilbride 7 E2
West Linton 8 B2
Westness 23 E2
Westnewton 3 E2
West Tarbert 24 A3
Westruther 9 D2
Westside 24 B3
West Tarbert 6 C2
West Yell 22 B2
Wetheral 3 F2
Whalton 4 C1
Whauphill 2 B2
Wheatley Hill 5 D2
Whickham 4 C2
Whifflet 25 F2
Whitburn *W.Loth.* 8 A2
Whitby *N.Yorks.* 5 F3
Whitecairns 24 C1
Whitecraig 8 C1
Whitecraig 25 F4
Whitehall 23 F2
Whitehaven 3 D3
Whitehills 17 E2
Whiterashes 17 E4
Whithorn 2 B2
Whiting Bay 7 D3
Whitley Bay 5 D1
Whittingham 9 E4
Wick *High.* 19 F2
Wigton 3 F2
Wigtown 2 B2
Willington *Dur.* 4 C3
Winchburgh 8 B1
Windermere 4 A4
Windygates 13 D4
Wingate 5 D2
Winston 4 C3
Winton 4 B3
Wishaw *N.Lan.* 8 A2
Wishaw *N.Lan.* 25 F3
Witton Gilbert 4 C2
Wolsingham 4 C2
Woodhaven 24 B5
Woodland 4 C3
Woodside 24 C2
Wooler 9 E3
Workington 3 E3
Wormit 13 D3
Wormit 24 A5
Wrelton 5 F4

Y

Yarm 5 D3
Yarrow 8 C3
Yoker 25 D2

CAPITAL

Plumbing, Heating & Building Services

28 Parsons Green Terrace, Edinburgh EH8 7AF

Service and Enquiries 0131 659 6491 (5 Lines 24-Hour) Fax: 0131 661 6173

A Company Assigned to Quality

Date	Time	Nature of Call		
		A	B	C

Job Ref. No.	Telephone No.	Account to:
Address	Work	
	Home	
	Other	

Works Description

Operative's Comments

Material Stock	Material from Supplier's Purchase Order No.

Client's Signature of Approval of Materials and Labour	
	Arrives
Client's Comments	Departs
Operative's Name(s)	Time Taken

Multiprint 6/95/908A

CAPITAL

Plumbing, Heating & Building Services

25 Saleona Green Terrace, Edinburgh EH8 7AP

Service and enquiries 0131 558 8491 (6 Lines 24 Hour) Fax 0131 557 6175

A Company Assigned to Quality

Date		Time			Nature of Call	
Job Ref. No.		Telephone No.			A	B
Address		Work		Accidental		
		Home				
		Other				

Works Description

Operative's Comments

Material Stock		Material from Suppliers Purchase Order No.	

Client's Signature of Approval of Materials and Labour

Client's Comments			Arrived
			Depart
Operative's Name(s)			Time Taken

CAPITAL

Plumbing, Heating & Building Services

LEAD CONTRACTORS ASSOCIATION

28 Parsons Green Terrace, Edinburgh EH8 7AF

Service and Enquiries 0131 659 6491 (5 Lines 24-Hour) Fax: 0131 661 6173

A Company Assigned to Quality

Date	Time	Nature of Call		
		A	B	C

Job Ref. No.	Telephone No.	Account to:
Address	Work	
	Home	
	Other	

Works Description

Operative's Comments

Material Stock	Material from Supplier's Purchase Order No.

Client's Signature of Approval of Materials and Labour

	Arrives
Client's Comments	Departs
Operative's Name(s)	Time Taken

Multiprint 6/95/908A

CAPITAL

Plumbing Heating & Building Services

28 Parsons Green Terrace, Edinburgh EH8 7AB

Service and Enquiries 0131 665 0691 (5 Lines 24 Hour) Fax 0131 661 6172

A Company Assured in Quality

Date			Time		Nature of Call	
						A	B
Job Ref. No.			Telephone No.		Account To.	
Address			Work			
			Home			
			Other			

Work Description

Operative's Comments

Material Siles	Material from Supplier/Purchase Order No.		

Client's Signature of Approval of Materials and Labour

Client's Comments		Arrive	
		Departs	
Operative's Name(s)		Time Taken	

Abbreviations used in city plan indexes

Aber.	Aberdeen
All.	Alley
App.	Approach
Ar.	Arcade
Av.	Avenue
Bdy.	Broadway
Blds.	Buildings
Bldgs.	Buildings
Boul.	Boulevard
Bri.	Bridge
Cft.	Croft
Circ.	Circus
Clo.	Close
Cor.	Corner
Cotts.	Cottages
Cres.	Crescent
Ct.	Court
Dr.	Drive
Dri.	Drive
E.	East
Est.	Estate
Gdns.	Gardens
Gra.	Grange
Grn.	Green
Gro.	Grove
Ho.	House
Ind.	Industrial
La.	Lane
Lr.	Lower
Manno.	Mannofield
Mans.	Mansions
Mkt.	Market
Ms.	Mews
Mt.	Mount
N.	North
Nth.	North
O.Aber.	Old Aberdeen
Par.	Parade
Pas.	Passage
Pk.	Park
Pl.	Place
Prom.	Promenade
Quad.	Quadrant
Rd.	Road
Ri.	Rise
S.	South
Sq.	Square
St.	Street
Sta.	Station
Sth.	South
Ter.	Terrace
Trd.	Trading
Vills.	Villas
Vw.	View
W.	West
Wf.	Wharf
Wk.	Walk
Wood.	Woodside
Yd.	Yard

A street name followed by the name of another street in italics does not appear on the map but will be found adjoining or near the latter.

ABERDEEN
32-35 Plan
36-37 Index

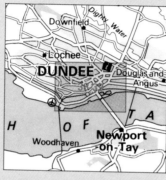

DUNDEE
38-39 Plan
40-41 Index

EDINBURGH
42-49 Plan
50-55 Index

GLASGOW
56-65 Plan
66-72 Index

ABERDEEN · DUNDEE · EDINBURGH · GLASGOW

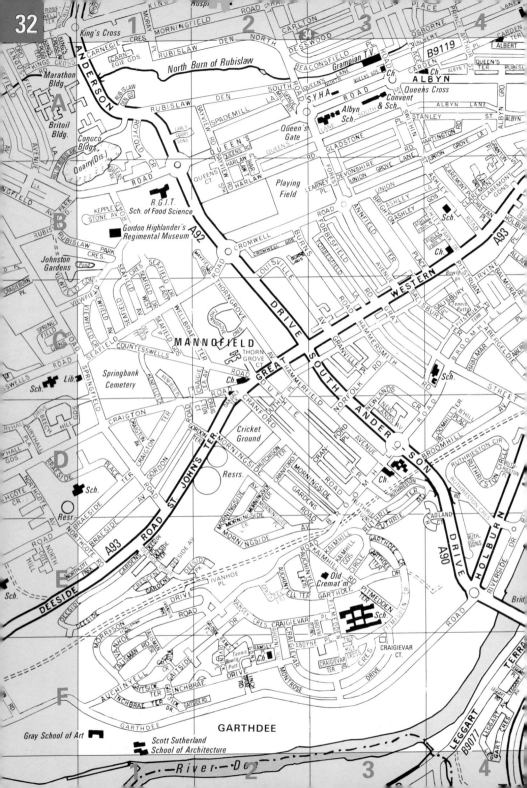

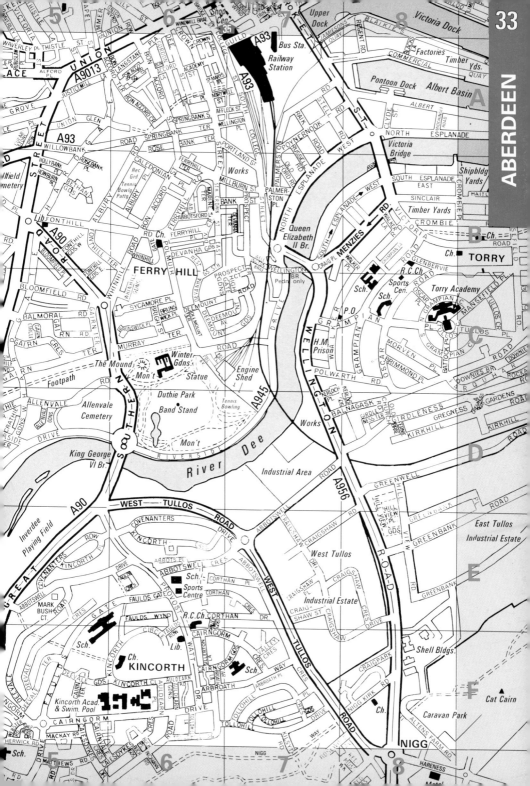

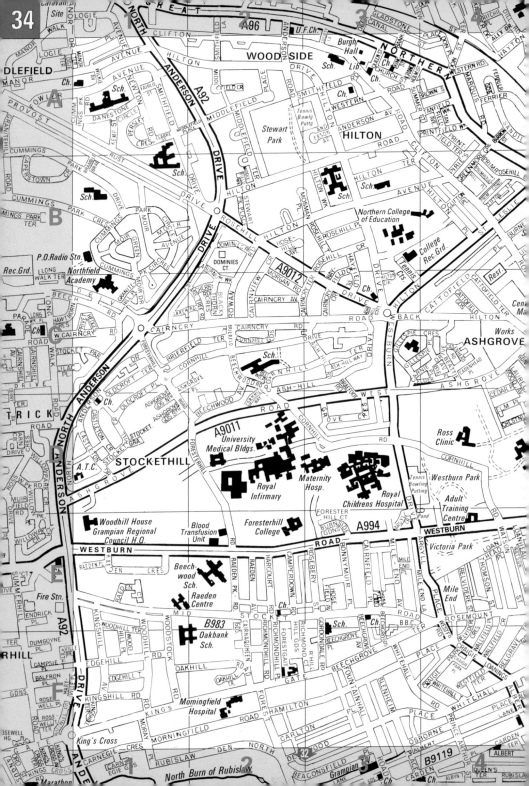

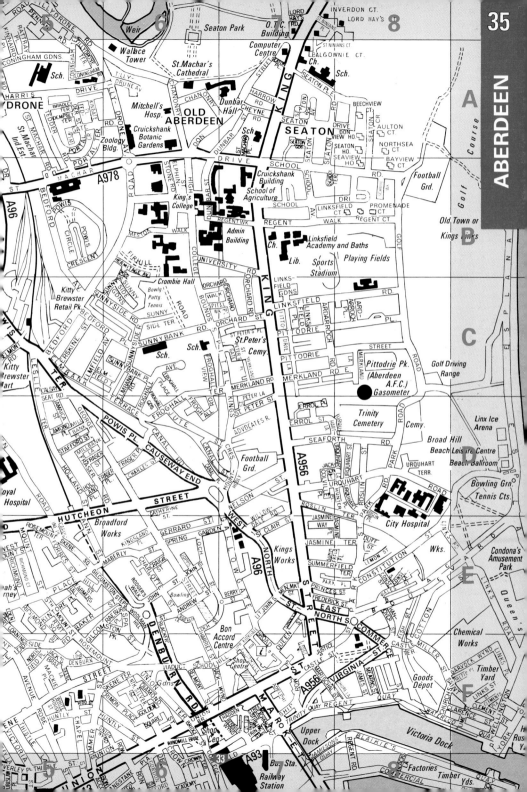

INDEX TO STREET NAMES

33 E6 Abbots Pl.
33 B6 Abbotsford La.
33 B6 Abbotsford Pl.
33 E7 Abbotswell Cres.
33 E5 Abbotswell Dr.
33 E7 Abbotswell Rd.
32 C4 Abergeldie Rd.
32 C4 Abergeldie Ter.
32 E3 Aboyne Gdns.
32 F2 Aboyne Pl.
32 E2 Aboyne Rd.
33 A6 Academy St.
35 F7 Adelphi
35 D7 Advocates Rd.
33 A6 Affleck Pl.
   Marywell St.
32 A6 Affleck St.
32 A3 Albert La.
33 F4 Albert Pl.
33 A8 Albert Quay
34 F4 Albert St.
32 A4 Albert Ter.
32 A4 Albert Wk.
   Albert St.
33 B6 Albury Gdns.
34 C2 Albury Rd.
   Albury Rd.
33 B6 Albury Pl.
33 B5 Albury Rd.
32 A4 Albyn Gro.
32 A4 Albyn La.
34 F3 Albyn Pl.
32 A4 Albyn Pl.
33 C5 Albyn Ter.
34 A4 Alexander Ter.
33 A5 Alford La.
   Alford Pl.
33 A5 Alford Pl.
32 B4 Allan St.
33 D5 Allenvale Gdns.
33 D5 Allenvale Rd.
33 F8 Altens Fm. Rd.
34 A3 Anderson Av.
35 E5 Ann St.
32 B3 Annfield Ter.
33 F6 Arbroath La.
33 F7 Arbroath Pl.
33 F6 Arbroath Way
35 C8 Ardarroch Pl.
35 C7 Ardarroch Rd.
34 E3 Argyll Cres.
34 E4 Argyll Pl.
34 C3 Ashgrove Rd.
   Back Hilton Rd.
34 D1 Ashgrove Gdns. N.
34 D1 Ashgrove Gdns. S.
34 C1 Ashgrove Pl.
34 C4 Ashgrove Rd.
34 D1 Ashgrove Rd. W.
34 C2 Ashhill Dr.
34 C3 Ashhill Rd.
34 C3 Ashhill Way
32 B3 Ashley Gdns.
32 B3 Ashley La.
32 B4 Ashley Pk. Dr.
32 B3 Ashley Pk. N.
32 B4 Ashley Pk. S.
32 B4 Ashley Rd.
33 A5 Ashvale Ct.
   Cuparstone Row
34 Ashvale Pl.
32 E2 Auchinyell Gdns.
32 F1 Auchinyell Rd.
32 E2 Auchinyell Ter.
35 C7 Auckland Pl.
   Merkland Rd.
33 F6 Auldearn Gdns.
33 F6 Auldearn Pl.
33 F6 Auldearn Rd.
35 A8 Aulton Ct.

B
34 C3 Back Hilton Rd.
33 F6 Back Wynd
35 E5 Baker Pl.
   Baker St.
35 E5 Baker St.
35 A7 Balgownie Ct.
33 C5 Balmoral Ct.
   South Mile End
32 B4 Balmoral Pl.
32 C5 Balmoral Rd.
32 C4 Balmoral Ter.
35 F8 Baltic St.
   Miller St.
33 B6 Bank St. (Ferry Hill)
34 A3 Bank St. (Hilton)
35 E8 Bannermill St.
   Cotton St.
32 A4 Barron St.
35 F8 Bath St.
   Windmill Brae
33 C8 Battock Pl.
35 A8 Bayview Ct.
32 A2 Bayview Rd.
32 B2 Bayview Rd. S.
35 A7 Beach Boul.
32 C6 Beaconsfield Pl.
32 A4 Beattie Av.
35 Beattie Pl.
35 B5 Bedford Av.

35 C5 Bedford Pl.
34 E3 Beechgrove Av.
34 E3 Beechgrove Gdns.
35 F7 Beechgrove Pl.
35 F7 Beechview Ct.
32 A1 Beechwood Av.
34 D2 Beechwood Av.
34 D1 Beechwood Ct.
   Castleton Dr.
34 C3 Beechwood Rd.
34 C2 Beechwood Rd.
34 C3 Belgrave Ter.
35 E5 Belmont Gdns.
35 C5 Belmont Rd.
35 F6 Belmont St.
35 E5 Belvidere Cres.
34 E4 Belvidere St.
35 F7 Berry St.
35 F8 Berryden Rd.
34 D1 Bethany Gdns.
34 C2 Birch Rd.
   Rowan Rd.
34 D1 Blackfriars St.
33 A8 Blacks La.
34 C2 Blackthorn Cres.
33 F8 Blaikies Quay
34 C4 Blenheim La.
   Blenheim Pl.
34 D6 Blenheim La.
34 D4 Blenheim Pl.
33 B5 Bloomfield Pl.
35 F5 Bloomfield Rd.
35 D6 Boa Vista Pl.
35 E6 Boddie Pl.
   Urquhart Rd.
34 A6 Bon Accord Cres.
34 C2 Bon Accord Cres. La.
   Bon Accord Cres.
34 A6 Bon Accord La.
33 F8 Bon Accord Sq.
   Bon Accord St.
34 A6 Bon Accord St.
34 A3 Bon Accord St.
34 A6 Bon Accord Ter.
35 A5 Bonnymuir Pl.
35 A5 Bradley Ter.
34 C3 Braefoot Rd.
32 C4 Braemar Pl.
32 E1 Braeside Av.
32 D1 Braeside Ter.
34 A1 Bramble Brae
35 B6 Brewery La.
   High St.
34 B4 Bridge Pl.
   Bridge St.
34 B4 Bridge St.
35 B6 Brierfield Rd.
33 B6 Brierfield Ter.
35 E8 Bright St.
35 B3 Brighton Pl.
35 A8 Brimmond Pl.
35 Broad St.
35 F7 Broomhill Av.
32 C4 Broomhill Pk.
   Broomhill Rd.
35 A5 Broomhill Pl.
35 A5 Broomhill Rd.
35 A5 Broomhill Ter.
35 E8 Brough Pl.
   Carnie Dr.
34 C1 Brunswick Pl.
33 C6 Buchanan Pl.
34 D3 Burnett Pl.
34 C3 Burns Gdns.
32 B2 Burns Rd.
34 E3 Burnside Gdns.

C
34 C4 Cadenhead Pl.
33 E6 Cadenhead Rd.
33 E6 Caiesdykes Dr.
34 F2 Cairncry Rd.
34 E8 Cairnaqueen Gdns.
34 C2 Cairncry Av.
34 C1 Cairncry Ct.
   Brierfield Ter.
34 C3 Cairncry Cres.
34 C2 Cairncry Rd.
34 E3 Cairnfield Pl.
33 F6 Cairnfield Pl.
33 F6 Cairngorm Cres.
33 F5 Cairngorm Dr.
35 E6 Cairngorm Gdns.
   Cairnvale Cres.
32 E2 Cairngorm Pl.
33 F5 Cairngorm Rd.
32 F2 Cairnvale Cres.
32 F2 Cairnvale Ter.
32 F3 Cairnview Ter.
34 C4 Caledonian La.
   Caledonian Pl.
34 A2 Caledonian Pl.
35 C5 Caledonian Pl.
34 E2 Camperdown Rd.
34 E7 Canal Pl.
34 D6 Canal Rd.
34 D6 Canal St.
35 E6 Candlemakers La.
   Loch St.

32 A3 Carden Pl.
34 F4 Carden Ter.
32 F2 Carlton Pl.
35 F7 Carmelite La.
   Carmelite St.
35 F7 Carmelite St.
32 A1 Carnegie Cres.
32 A1 Carnegies Brae
   Flourmill La.
32 B2 Carnie Dr.
32 B2 Carnie Gdns.
   Carnie La.
33 A6 Caroline Apts.
   Forbes St.
33 A6 Caroline Pl.
   Hanover St.
33 A6 Castle Hill
34 B1 Castle St.
34 A1 Castle Ter.
33 A5 Castleton Cres.
   Castleton Dr.
33 D6 Catherine St.
34 C4 Cattofield Gdns.
34 C4 Cattofield Pl.
34 C4 Cattofield Ter.
34 D6 Causewayend
33 A6 Cedar Pl.
33 C6 Chanonry
35 F5 Chapel St.
35 D6 Charles St.
35 E6 Charlotte Pl.
   Charlotte St.
32 E1 Charlotte St.
32 B4 Chattan Pl.
34 C2 Cherry Rd.
34 D4 Chestnut Row
34 A7 Cheyne Rd.
33 F8 Church St. (Footdee)
33 F5 Church St. (Woodside)
33 F5 Church Wk.
   High St.
34 B4 Claremont Gdns.
32 A2 Claremont Gro.
34 B6 Claremont Pl.
34 B4 Claremont St.
33 B6 Clarke St.
   Dunbar St.
34 B6 Clifton La.
34 B4 Clifton Pl.
33 A8 Clyde St.
33 B7 College Bounds
32 F2 College St.
35 F6 Colville Pl.
35 E8 Commerce St.
35 A8 Commercial Quay
35 F7 Concert Ct.
   Broad St.
34 B2 Coningham Gdns.
35 A5 Coningham Rd.
35 A5 Coningham Ter.
35 E8 Constitution La.
35 E5 Constitution St.
32 C2 Cornhill Ct.
33 E6 Cornhill Dr.
35 E8 Cornhill Gdns.
35 E8 Cornhill Rd.
35 B6 Cornhill Sq.
   Ashhill Rd.
32 C2 Cornhill Ter.
35 Cornhill Way
35 F7 Correction Wynd
   Union St.
33 E6 Corthan Cres.
33 E6 Corthan Dr.
33 E6 Corthan Pl.
33 E6 Cotton St.
35 E7 Cottage Brae
35 E7 Covenanters Dr.
33 E7 Covenanters Row
34 E7 Craibstone La.
   Bon Accord La.
33 B7 Craig Pl.
33 F4 Craigie Loanings
34 F4 Craigie Pk.
34 D4 Craigie Pk. Pl.
34 E6 Craigie St.
34 C5 Craigiebuckler Av.
33 C5 Craigiebuckler Ter.
   Craigievar Cres.
34 C5 Craigievar Cres.
33 D7 Craigievar Pl.
32 F2 Craigievar Rd.
   Montrose Dr.
34 C5 Craigievar Ter.
35 F7 Craigpark
33 E7 Craigshaw Cres.
33 E7 Craigshaw Dr.
33 E7 Craigshaw Pl.
33 E7 Craigshaw Rd.
33 E7 Craigshaw St.
32 D1 Craigton Av.
32 D2 Craigton Ct.

32 D1 Craigton Rd.
32 D1 Craigton Ter.
32 D3 Cranford Pl.
32 D2 Cranford Rd.
32 D2 Cranford Ter.
33 D5 Crathie Gdns. W.
33 F6 Crimon Pl.
33 B8 Crombie Rd.
32 B3 Cromwell Ct.
   Forbesfield Rd.
32 B2 Cromwell Gdns.
32 B3 Cromwell Rd.
33 A6 Crooked La.
   Crown Ter.
33 A6 Crown St.
35 E8 Crown St.
33 B6 Crown Ter.
34 B1 Cummings Pk. Circ.
34 A1 Cummings Pk. Rd.
34 A5 Cuparstone Ct.
   Cuparstone Row
33 A5 Cuparstone La.
   Cuparstone Row
33 A5 Cuparstone Row

D
34 A1 Danestone Circle
32 C1 Dee Pl.
32 F2 Dee St.
33 C6 Deemount Av.
33 C6 Deemount Gdns.
33 C6 Deemount Ter.
32 C6 Deeside Av.
32 E1 Deeside Cres.
32 E1 Deeside Dr.
32 D6 Deeside Gdns.
32 C6 Deeside Pk.
32 D6 Deeside Ter.
32 A5 Deevale Cres.
32 F5 Deevale Rd.
35 F6 Deevale Ter.
35 A5 Dempsey Ter.
   Belmont St.
33 E6 Denburn Rd.
32 A2 Desswood Pl.
33 C5 Devanha Cres.
33 C5 Devanha Gdns.
33 C5 Devanha Gdns. E.
32 C5 Devanha Gdns. S.
32 F1 Devanha Gdns. W.
32 F1 Devanha La.
   Devanha Gdns.
32 E2 Devanha Ter.
32 B7 Devenick Pl.
32 B3 Devonshire Rd.
32 E7 Diamond La.
   Diamond St.
32 E3 Diamond Pl.
32 F1 Diamond St.
32 E3 Dominies Ct.
35 D5 Dominies Rd.
35 E6 Dominies Ter.
34 A4 Don Pl.
35 F5 Donald Pl.
   Forbes St.
35 F5 Donview Ho.
35 F5 Douglas La.
   High St.
35 E5 Duff St.
35 B6 Dunbar St.
34 C3 Duncans Pl.
33 D8 Duthie Ct.
33 D8 Duthie Pl.
33 D8 Duthie Ter.

E
35 F6 Earls Gdns.
35 B6 East Craibstone St.
   Bon Accord St.
35 F7 East Grn.
   Hadden St.
34 F1 East N. St.
34 F1 Eden Pl.
34 F3 Edgehill Rd.
34 B8 Edgehill Ter.
32 C4 Elm Pl.
34 A3 Elmbank Rd.
34 C1 Elmbank Ter.
34 A4 Elmfield Av.
34 B6 Elmfield Pl.
   High St.
32 B1 Elphinstone Rd.
32 C3 Errol Pl.
32 C3 Errol St.
35 E5 Erskine St.
34 E4 Esslemont Av.
35 F7 Exchange La.
   Exchange St.
35 F7 Exchange St.
35 F7 Exchequer Row
   Ship Row

F
34 A1 Fairlie St.

35 E5 Farmers Hall La.
35 E7 Farrier La.
   Mealmarket St.
33 E6 Faulds Cres.
33 F5 Faulds Gate
33 F6 Faulds Row
33 E6 Faulds Wynd
35 F7 Fernie Brae
34 F2 Ferrier Cres.
32 C2 Ferrier Gdns.
32 C3 Ferryhill Gdns.
   Ferryhill Ter.
35 E8 Ferryhill Pl.
34 E2 Ferryhill Rd.
33 B5 Ferryhill Ter.
32 B2 Firhill Rd.
33 B6 Fish St.
35 E8 Fonthill Gdns. E.
34 A7 Fonthill Gdns. W.
32 A4 Fonthill Rd.
35 D8 Fonthill Ter.
   Urquhart Pl.
34 C3 Forbesfield La.
34 B3 Forbesfield Rd.
34 A4 Forest Av.
32 E4 Forest Rd.
34 E3 Foresterhill Ct.
34 C1 Foresterhill Rd.
32 F2 Forestgait
34 A5 Fountainhall Rd.
34 F3 Fraser Pl.
34 D6 Fraser Rd.
33 D8 Fraser St.
33 D8 Fraser St.
35 C6 Frederick St.
33 D6 Froghall Av.
   Spital
34 E3 Froghall Gdns.
34 C3 Froghall Pl.
34 B2 Froghall Rd.
   Stewart Pk. Pl.
34 A3 Froghall Ter.
34 B4 Froghall Vw.

G
35 F6 Gaelic La.
   Belmont St.
33 B3 Gairn Circle
33 C5 Gairn Ct.
   Gairn Ter.
33 C5 Gairn Rd.
34 E4 Gairn Ter.
34 E3 Gaitside Cres.
34 E3 Gaitside Dr.
34 B5 Gaitside Pl.
35 D8 Gaitside Rd.
34 E7 Gallowgate
35 E5 Garthdee Cres.
   Garthdee Dr.
32 E3 Garthdee Gdns.
   Garthdee Ter.
32 E3 Garthdee Rd.
35 D5 George St.
32 F5 Gerrard St.
32 F1 Gilcomston Ct.
   Kidd St.
35 F5 Gilcomston Land
   Kidd St.
35 B4 Gilcomston Pk.
35 F1 Gilcomston Steps
   Farmers Hall La.
34 C3 Gillespie Cres.
35 F5 Gillespie Pl.
33 D8 Girdleness Rd.
33 D8 Girdleness Ter.
32 D2 Gladstone Pl.
33 B8 Glenbervie Rd.
33 A5 Glendale Ms.
   Union Glen
35 F6 Golden Sq.
34 B6 Gordon Rd.
32 D1 Gordon St.
32 D2 Gordon Ter.
   Gordondale Rd.
34 F3 Gordondale Rd.
34 B8 Grampian La.
32 C7 Grampian Pl.
34 A3 Grampian Rd.
32 E3 Grandholm St.
34 A4 Granton Pl.
34 B6 Grants Pl.
   High St.
32 A2 Granville Pl.
32 C3 Gray St.
35 E5 Great Southern Rd.
32 A4 Great Western Pl.
33 A4 Great Western Rd.
35 F7 Green, The
35 E6 Greenbank Cres.
35 E8 Greenbank Pl.
35 E8 Greenbank Rd.
35 B4 Greenmore Gdns.
35 C7 Greenwell Rd.

35 E5 Greig Ct.
   Hutcheon St.
35 E5 Grosvenor Pl.
34 D3 Grove Cres.
33 A7 Guild St.

H
35 F7 Hadden St.
34 F2 Hamilton Pl.
32 C2 Hammerfield Av.
32 C3 Hammersmith Rd.
35 E5 Hanover St.
32 B2 Harcourt Rd.
32 B2 Harlaw Pl.
32 B2 Harlaw Rd.
32 B2 Harlaw Ter.
35 F6 Harriet St.
35 A5 Harris Dr.
34 A7 Harrow Rd.
32 A4 Hartington Rd.
35 D8 Hawthorn Ter.
   Urquhart Pl.
34 C3 Hayfield Cres.
34 B3 Hayfield Pl.
34 A4 Hayton Rd.
32 E4 Headland Ct.
34 B6 Hermitage Av.
33 F5 Hetherwick Rd.
35 B6 High St.
33 C7 Highgate Gdns.
33 E5 Hill St.
34 A5 Hill St.
34 D8 Hill Vw. Cres.
34 D8 Hill Vw. Dr.
33 D8 Hill Vw. Rd.
35 C6 Hillhead Ter.
   Spital
34 C3 Hilton Av.
34 C3 Hilton Circle
34 B2 Hilton Ct.
34 A3 Hilton Dr.
34 B4 Hilton Pl.
34 B2 Hilton Rd.
34 A3 Hilton St.
34 B3 Hilton Ter.
34 B3 Hilton Wk.
33 C5 Holburn Pl.
33 C5 Holburn Rd.
33 B4 Holburn St.
32 E4 Holburn St.
33 D5 Holland Pl.
33 C5 Holland St.
33 B5 Hollybank Pl.
34 E3 Hosefield Av.
33 B5 Hosefield Rd.
35 D8 Howburn Pl.
33 B6 Hunter Pl.
35 F5 Huntly St.
35 E5 Hutcheon Ct.
   Hutcheon St.
34 D2 Hutcheon Ter.
35 E5 Hutcheon St.

I
35 F7 Imperial Pl.
   Stirling St.
32 F1 Inchbrae Dr.
32 F2 Inchbrae Rd.
32 F1 Inchbrae Ter.
32 B4 Irvine Pl.
32 E2 Ivanhoe Pl.
32 F1 Ivanhoe Rd.
32 E1 Ivanhoe Wk.

J
35 F5 Jacks Brae
35 D7 Jackson Ter.
35 D5 Jamaica St.
33 B8 James St.
33 A7 Jamiesons Quay
35 E8 Jasmine Pl.
35 E7 Jasmine Ter.
35 E7 Jasmine Way
32 E6 John St.
35 E6 Jopps La.
34 A5 Justice Mill Brae
   Justice Mill La.
33 A5 Justice Mill La.
35 F7 Justice St.
35 D6 Jute St.

K
32 E3 Kaimhill Circle
34 A3 Kaimhill Gdns.
32 E3 Kaimhill Rd.
34 A1 Kemp St.
32 C1 Kenfield Cres.
32 C1 Kenfield Pl.
32 B1 Kepplestone Av.
32 C8 Kerloch Gdns.
32 C7 Kerloch Pl.
35 F5 Kidd St.
35 F7 Kilsyth Rd.
35 E6 Kincorth Circle
35 E8 Kincorth Cres.
35 E8 Kincorth Gdns.
35 D8 Kincorth Pl.
35 D6 King George VI Bri.
35 C7 King St. (Aberdeen)

37
ABERDEEN

34 A3 King St. (Woodside)
35 D7 Kings Cres.
34 E1 Kingshill Av.
34 F1 Kingshill Rd.
34 F1 Kingshill Ter.
35 E6 Kingsland Pl.
35 E5 Kintore Gdns.
Kintore Pl.
35 E5 Kintore Pl.
33 D8 Kirkhill Rd.

L

34 B2 Laburnum Wk.
35 D5 Lamond Pl.
33 A6 Langstane Pl.
34 C1 Larch Rd.
34 C4 Laurel Wd. Av.
35 F5 Leadside Rd.
32 B3 Learney Pl.
32 F4 Leggart Av.
32 F4 Leggart Cres.
32 F4 Leggart Pl.
32 F4 Leggart Rd.
32 F4 Leggart Ter.
35 E8 Lemon Pl.
Park St.
35 E8 Lemon St.
34 B4 Leslie Rd.
34 C5 Leslie Ter.
34 B4 Lilybank Pl.
35 F6 Lindsay St.
Golden Sq.
35 E8 Links Rd.
35 B7 Linksfield Ct.
35 C7 Linksfield Gdns.
35 C7 Linksfield Pl.
35 C7 Linksfield Rd.
35 F6 Little Belmont St.
Belmont St.
35 F5 Little Chapel St.
Chapel St.
35 E7 Little John St.
34 E4 Loanhead Pl.
34 E4 Loanhead Ter.
34 E4 Loanhead Wk.
Loanhead Ter.
35 E6 Loch St.
35 F7 Lodge Wk.
32 B2 Louisville Av.

M

35 E6 Maberley St.
33 F5 Mackay Rd.
35 B6 Mackenzie Pl.
High St.
35 F5 Mackie Pl.
35 E5 Magdala Pl.
Short Loanings
34 A1 Manor Ter.
32 D4 Margaret Pl.
Ruthrieston Circle
35 F5 Margaret St.
Rose St.
33 B6 Marine Ct.
Marine Ter.
33 B6 Marine Pl.
South Crown St.
33 B6 Marine Ter.
35 F7 Marischal Ct.
Justice St.
35 F7 Marischal St.
33 E5 Mark Bush Ct.
Abbotswell Dr.
35 B6 Market La.
High St.
35 F7 Market St.
34 A4 Marquis Rd.
35 F7 Martins La.
Carmelite St.
33 A6 Marywell St.
32 B2 Mayfield Gdns.
33 A5 McCombies Ct.
Union St.
35 E7 Mealmarket St.
35 F8 Mearns St.
33 C7 Menzies Rd.
35 C8 Merkland La.
35 C7 Merkland Pl.
35 C7 Merkland Rd.
35 C7 Merkland Rd. E.
35 B6 Meston Wk.
34 E2 Mid Stocket Rd.
33 A8 Midchingle Rd.
34 A2 Middlefield Cres.
34 A2 Middlefield Pl.
34 A2 Middlefield Ter.
34 B2 Middlefield Wk.
34 E3 Mile End Av.
34 E3 Mile End La.
34 E3 Mile End Pl.
35 D5 Millbank La.
35 D5 Millbank Pl.
33 B6 Millburn St.
35 F8 Miller St.
35 F5 Minister La.
Summer St.
34 B1 Moir Av.
34 B1 Moir Cres.
34 C1 Moir Dr.
34 B1 Moir Grn.
32 F2 Montrose Dr.
34 F1 Moray Pl.
34 C2 Morgan Rd.
34 F1 Morningfield Rd.
32 E2 Morningside Av.
32 E2 Morningside Cres.
32 D2 Morningside Gdns.
32 D2 Morningside Gro.
Morningside Rd.
32 D2 Morningside Pl.
32 D2 Morningside Rd.
32 D2 Morningside Ter.
32 F1 Morrison Dr.
33 C8 Morven Pl.
34 B2 Mosman Gdns.
34 A2 Mosman Pl.
35 D7 Mount Hooly
35 E5 Mount St.
35 E5 Mountview Gdns.
Mount St.
33 C6 Murray Ter.

N

32 B4 Nellfield Pl.
35 D7 Nelson Ct.
King St.
35 D7 Nelson La.
Nelson St.
35 D7 Nelson St.
35 F7 Netherkirkgate
Union St.
32 D3 Newlands Av.
32 D3 Newlands Cres.
34 A1 Newton Rd.
33 F8 Nigg Kirk Rd.
32 D3 Norfolk Rd.
33 A8 North Esp. E.
33 B7 North Esp. W.
33 C8 North Grampian Circle
35 E6 North St. Andrew St.
St. Andrew St.
35 F6 North Silver St.
35 F5 Northfield Pl.
35 A8 Northsea Ct.
35 E5 Novar Pl.
Ann St.

O

32 D2 Oakdale Ter.
34 F2 Oakhill Cres.
34 F1 Oakhill Rd.
33 D8 Old Ch. Rd.
33 B7 Old Ford Rd.
34 D1 Oldcroft Ct.
Castleton Dr.
34 D1 Oldcroft Pl.
34 C1 Oldcroft Ter.
33 B6 Oldmill Rd.
Bon Accord St.
35 C7 Orchard La.
Orchard Pl.
35 C7 Orchard Pl.
35 C7 Orchard Rd.
35 C7 Orchard St.
35 C6 Orchard Wk.
34 F3 Osborne Pl.
33 C8 Oscar Pl.
33 C8 Oscar Rd.

P

33 B7 Palmerston Pl.
33 B7 Palmerston Rd.
35 E7 Park Pl.
35 D8 Park Rd.
35 E8 Park St.
35 F6 Patagonian Ct.
Belmont St.
35 E7 Peacocks Clo.
East N. St.
34 A1 Persley Cres.
34 B4 Piries La.
32 E3 Pitmedden Cres.
32 E3 Pitmedden Rd.
32 E3 Pitmedden Ter.
32 B4 Pitstruan Pl.
32 C4 Pitstruan Ter.
35 C7 Pittodrie La.
35 C7 Pittodrie Pl.
35 C7 Pittodrie St.
34 C2 Plane Tree Rd.
33 C6 Polmuir Av.
33 C6 Polmuir Pl.
33 B6 Polmuir Rd.
33 C7 Polwarth Rd.
34 C1 Poplar Rd.
Larch Rd.
35 A5 Portal Cres.
35 B5 Portal Ter.
35 E7 Porthill Ct.
Gallowgate
33 A6 Portland St.
35 F7 Poultry Mkt. La.
Queen St.
35 B5 Powis Circle
35 B5 Powis Cres.
35 D6 Powis Pl.
35 C5 Powis Ter.
33 A7 Poynernook Rd.
34 B4 Primrosehill Dr.
34 B4 Primrosehill Gdns.
34 B4 Primrosehill Pl.
34 F4 Prince Arthur St.
35 E7 Princes St.
34 A4 Printfield Ter.
34 A4 Printfield Wk.
34 C1 Privet Hedges
35 B8 Promenade Ct.
33 C6 Prospect Ct.
33 B7 Prospect Ter.
33 E6 Provost Watt Dr.

Q

35 F7 Queen St. (Aberdeen)
34 A3 Queen St. (Hilton)
32 B1 Queens Av.
32 B2 Queens Ct.
32 A3 Queens Gdns.
32 A3 Queens La. N.
32 A2 Queens La. S.
32 A4 Queens Ter.

R

35 E6 Raeburn Pl.
34 E2 Raeden Av.
34 E1 Raeden Ct.
34 E1 Raeden Cres.
34 E2 Raeden Pk. Rd.
34 E1 Raeden Pl.
33 A7 Raik Rd.
32 E2 Ramsay Cres.
32 F2 Ramsay Gdns.
32 F2 Ramsay Pl.
35 B8 Regent Ct.
35 F8 Regent Quay
35 F8 Regent Rd.
35 B7 Regent Wk.
35 F7 Rennies Wynd
35 E5 Richmond Ct.
35 E5 Richmond St.
35 E5 Richmond Ter.
35 E5 Richmond Wk.
Richmond St.
34 F3 Richmondhill Ct.
34 F2 Richmondhill Gdns.
34 F2 Richmondhill Pl.
34 F2 Richmondhill Rd.
33 D6 Riverside Dr.
33 D5 Riverside Ter.
35 E6 Rodgers Wk.
35 F5 Rose Pl.
Rose St.
35 F5 Rose St.
33 B5 Rosebank Pl.
33 A6 Rosebank Ter.
34 E3 Rosebery St.
34 B2 Rosehill Av.
34 C1 Rosehill Ct.
Brierfield Ter.
34 B3 Rosehill Cres.
34 B2 Rosehill Dr.
34 B3 Rosehill Pl.
34 B3 Rosehill Ter.
34 E4 Rosemount Pl.
35 E5 Rosemount Sq.
35 E5 Rosemount Ter.
35 F5 Rosemount Viad.
35 D8 Roslin Pl.
35 D8 Roslin St.
35 D7 Roslin Ter.
34 C2 Rowan Rd.
32 A1 Royfold Cres.
32 A1 Rubislaw Den Gdns.
32 A1 Rubislaw Den N.
32 A1 Rubislaw Den S.
32 A5 Rubislaw Pl.
32 A4 Rubislaw Ter.
32 A4 Rubislaw Ter. La.
Rubislaw Ter.
35 F6 Ruby La.
North Silver St.
35 F6 Ruby Pl.
North Silver St.
33 A7 Russell Rd.
32 E4 Ruth Gdns.
32 D3 Ruthrie Gdns.
32 E3 Ruthrie Rd.
32 E3 Ruthrie Ter.
32 D4 Ruthrieston Circle
32 D4 Ruthrieston Cres.
32 D4 Ruthrieston Pl.
32 D3 Ruthrieston Rd.

S

35 E6 St. Andrew St.
33 A5 St. Catharines Wynd
Union St.
35 E7 St. Clair St.
33 A6 St. Johns Pl.
Academy St.
32 D1 St. Johns Ter.
35 B5 St. Machar Dr.
35 A7 St. Machar Pl.
35 A5 St. Machar Rd.
35 F6 St. Mary's Ct.
Union Wynd
33 A6 St. Marys Pl.
35 F7 St. Nicholas La.
Union St.
35 F7 St. Nicholas St.
Union St.
35 A7 St. Ninians Ct.
35 E7 St. Paul St.
Gallowgate
35 D7 St. Peter La.
35 D7 St. Peter St.
35 C7 St. Peters Gate
35 C7 St. Peters Pl.
32 A3 St. Swithin St.
32 C3 Salisbury Ct.
Salisbury Ter.
32 C4 Salisbury Pl.
32 C3 Salisbury Ter.
34 A4 Sandiland Dr.
35 B7 School Av.
35 B7 School Dr.
35 F6 School Hill
35 B7 School Rd.
35 B7 School Ter.
35 B8 School Wk.
32 B1 Seafield Av.
32 C1 Seafield Ct.
32 C1 Seafield Cres.
32 B1 Seafield Dr. E.
32 C1 Seafield Dr. W.
32 C1 Seafield Gdns.
32 C1 Seafield Rd.
35 D7 Seaforth Rd.
35 E7 Seamount Ct.
Gallowgate
35 E7 Seamount Rd.
Gallowgate
35 A7 Seaton Av.
35 A8 Seaton Cres.
35 A7 Seaton Dr.
35 A7 Seaton Gdns.
35 A8 Seaton Ho.
35 A7 Seaton Pl.
35 A7 Seaton Pl. E.
35 A7 Seaton Rd.
35 A7 Seaton Wk.
35 A8 Seaview Ho.
33 F5 Shepherd Pl.
35 F7 Ship Row
35 E7 Shoe La.
35 F7 Shore Brae
Ship Row
35 F8 Shore La.
35 E5 Short Loanings
33 F6 Sillerton La.
33 B8 Sinclair Rd.
35 F5 Skene La.
35 E5 Skene Sq.
35 F5 Skene St.
35 F6 Skene Ter.
34 A1 Smithfield Ct.
Fairlie St.
34 A1 Smithfield Dr.
34 A2 Smithfield La.
34 A3 Smithfield Rd.
34 A3 Society La.
32 C3 South Anderson Dr.
33 A7 South Coll. St.
35 E8 South Constitution St.
33 B6 South Crown St.
33 B8 South Esp. E.
33 B7 South Esp. W.
33 C8 South Grampian Circle
33 C5 South Mile End
35 E5 South Mt. St.
35 F6 South Silver St.
Union St.
34 C2 South Wk.
Ashhill Dr.
35 E6 Spa St.
32 A2 Spademill La.
32 A2 Spademill Rd.
35 C6 Spital
35 C6 Spital Wk.
35 E6 Spring Gdn.
33 A6 Springbank Pl.
Bon Accord St.
33 A6 Springbank St.
33 A6 Springbank Ter.
32 C1 Springfield Rd.
35 D5 Stafford St.
32 A3 Stanley St.
33 A7 Stell Rd.
35 F5 Stevenson Ct.
Upper Denburn
34 B2 Stewart Pk. Ct.
Stewart Pk. Pl.
34 B2 Stewart Pk. Pl.
35 F7 Stirling St.
34 D1 Stockethill Av.
Stockethill Cres.
34 C1 Stockethill Ct.
Foresterhill Rd.
34 D1 Stockethill Cres.
34 C1 Stockethill La.
Oldcroft Ter.
34 D1 Stockethill Pl.
Castleton Dr.
34 D1 Stockethill Sq.
Stockethill Cres.
34 C1 Stockethill Way
Oldcroft Ter.
35 F8 Sugarhouse La.
Mearns St.
35 F5 Summer St. (Aberdeen)
34 A3 Summer St. (Hilton)
35 E7 Summerfield Pl.
35 E7 Summerfield Ter.
35 C6 Sunnybank Pl.
35 C6 Sunnybank Rd.
35 C6 Sunnyside Av.
35 C6 Sunnyside Gdns.
35 C6 Sunnyside Rd.
35 C6 Sunnyside Ter.
35 C6 Sunnyside Wk.
Sunnybank Pl.
33 C6 Sycamore Pl.

T

32 F1 Talisman Dr.
32 F1 Talisman Rd.
32 E1 Talisman Wk.
34 A4 Tanfield Av.
34 A4 Tanfield Ct.
Tanfield Wk.
34 A4 Tanfield Wk.
35 A5 Tedder Rd.
35 A5 Tedder St.
35 F8 Theatre La.
Regent Quay
35 F5 Thistle Ct.
Rose St.
35 F5 Thistle La.
33 A5 Thistle Pl.
Thistle St.
33 A5 Thistle St.
35 B6 Thoms Ct.
High St.
35 B6 Thoms Pl.
High St.
34 E4 Thomson St.
32 C2 Thorngrove Av.
32 C2 Thorngrove Ct.
35 A6 Tillydrone Av.
35 A5 Tillydrone Ter.
33 F7 Tollohill Cres.
33 F7 Tollohill Dr.
33 F7 Tollohill Gdns.
33 F6 Tollohill La.
33 F7 Tollohill Pl.
33 F6 Tollohill Sq.
35 F7 Trinity La.
Exchange St.
35 F7 Trinity Quay
35 F7 Trinity St.
33 C8 Tullos Circle
32 F3 Two Mile Cross

U

35 F6 Union Bri.
33 A5 Union Glen
32 B3 Union Gro.
32 B3 Union Gro. Ct.
Union Gro.
32 A4 Union Gro. La.
33 A5 Union Row
33 A5 Union St.
35 F6 Union Ter.
35 F5 Union Wynd
35 B6 University Rd.
35 F5 Upper Denburn
35 F7 Upper Kirkgate
35 D8 Urquhart La.
35 D8 Urquhart Pl.
35 D8 Urquhart Rd.
35 D8 Urquhart St.
35 D8 Urquhart Ter.

V

33 F7 Valley Cres.
33 E6 Valley Gdns.
33 A8 Victoria Bri.
33 B8 Victoria Rd.
35 F5 Victoria St.
35 E5 View Ter.
32 C1 Viewfield Av.
32 C1 Viewfield Cres.
32 C1 Viewfield Rd.
35 F7 Virginia Ct.
Justice St.
35 F8 Virginia St.

W

35 B6 Wagrills La.
High St.
35 F8 Wales La.
Mearns St.
35 E8 Wales St.
33 B8 Walker La.
33 B8 Walker Pl.
33 C7 Walker Rd.
34 F4 Wallfield Cres.
34 F4 Wallfield Pl.
35 F8 Water La.
Mearns St.
35 F8 Waterloo Quay
34 E4 Watson La.
34 E4 Watson St.
35 F5 Waverley La.
33 A5 Waverley Pl.
33 F5 Webster Rd.
35 F8 Weighhouse Sq.
Virginia St.
32 C1 Wellbrae Ter.
33 B7 Wellington Brae
33 B7 Wellington Bri.
33 A6 Wellington Pl.
33 C7 Wellington Rd.
33 A6 West Craibstone St.
Bon Accord Ter.
35 E5 West Mt. St.
35 E7 West N. St.
33 D6 West Tullos Rd.
35 E5 Westburn Ct.
Westburn Rd.
34 C3 Westburn Dr.
34 E1 Westburn Rd.
34 A3 Western Rd.
34 F4 Westfield Rd.
34 F4 Westfield Ter.
33 C6 Whinhill Gdns.
33 B6 Whinhill Gate
33 C6 Whinhill Rd.
34 F4 Whitehall Pl.
34 F3 Whitehall Rd.
34 F4 Whitehall Ter.
35 F5 Whitehouse St.
34 A1 Wilkie Av.
33 A5 Willowbank Rd.
35 E7 Willowdale Pl.
35 F6 Windmill Brae
35 F6 Windmill La.
Windmill Brae
35 F5 Windsor Pl.
Victoria St.
35 A5 Wingate Pl.
35 A5 Wingate Rd.
34 D1 Woodhill Ct.
Castleton Dr.
34 F1 Woodhill Pl.
34 F1 Woodhill Rd.
34 E1 Woodhill Ter.
34 F1 Woodstock Rd.
35 E6 Woolmanhill
35 B6 Wright & Coopers Pl.
High St.

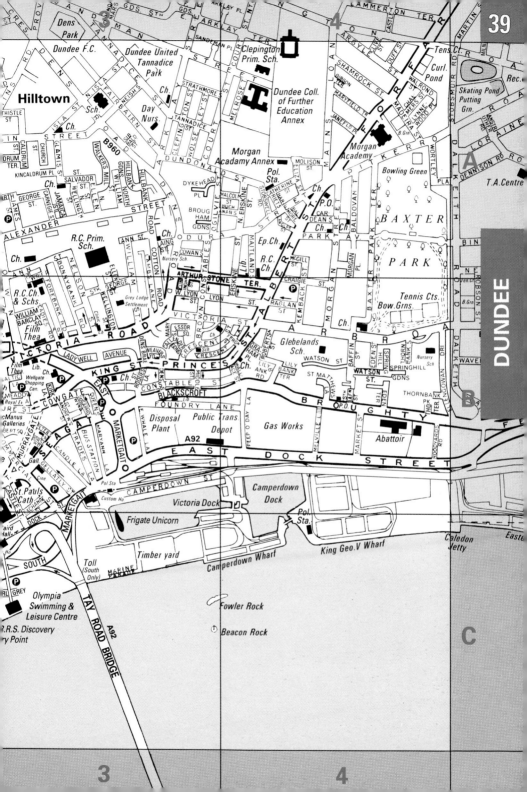

DUNDEE

Dens Park

Dundee F.C.

Dundee United
Tannadice
Park

Hilltown

Clepington
Prim. Sch.

Dundee Coll.
of Further
Education
Annex

Morgan
Academy

Morgan
Acadamy Annex

Pol.
Sta.

Curl.
Pond

Skating Pond
Putting
Grn.

Rec.

T.A. Centre

Bowling Green

BAXTER

PARK

Tennis Cts.
Bow.Grns.

R.C. Prim.
Sch.

William
Barclay
Film
Thea

R.C. Ch.
& Schs

Grey Lodge
Settlement

Glebelands
Sch.

VICTORIA ROAD

PRINCES STREET

KING STREET

Wellgate
Shopping Cen.

COWGATE

Blackscroft

FOUNDRY LANE

Disposal
Plant

Public Trans
Depot

Gas Works

Abattoir

EAST DOCK STREET

A92

Bus Station

Pol Sta.

McManus
Galleries

St Pauls
Cath.

Custom Ho.

Camperdown Dock

Victoria Dock

Pol.
Sta.

King Geo.V Wharf

Caledon
Jetty

Easte

Frigate Unicorn

Timber yard

Camperdown Wharf

Toll
(South
Only)

TAY ROAD BRIDGE

A92

Olympia
Swimming &
Leisure Centre

R.R.S. Discovery

Fowler Rock

Beacon Rock

SOUTH

A

B

C

3

4

40

INDEX TO STREET NAMES

38	A2	Adelaide Pl.
38	A2	Adelaide Ter.
38	C2	Airlie Pl.
38	A1	Albany Ter.
38	B3	Albert Sq.
39	B4	Albert St.
39	A3	Alexander St.
39	B3	Allan St.
38	A2	Alva Sq.
38	B1	Anchor La.
39	A3	Ann St.
38	B1	Annfield Rd.
38	B1	Annfield Row
38	B1	Annfield St.
39	B4	Arbroath Rd.
39	A4	Argyle St.
39	A3	Arklay St.
38	B2	Arthur St.
39	A3	Arthurstone Ter.
38	C2	Artillery La.
38	B1	Ash La.
		Ash St.
38	B2	Ash St.

B

39	B4	Baffin St.
39	B4	Baffin Ter.
		Baffin St.
39	A4	Baldovan Ter.
38	B1	Balfour St.
38	A1	Balgayview Gdns.
39	A4	Balmore St.
38	C1	Baltic Gdns.
		Patons La.
38	B3	Baltic La.
38	B1	Bank Mill Rd.
38	B2	Bank St.
38	A2	Barrack Rd.
38	B2	Barrack St.
38	A4	Baxter Pk.
39	B4	Baxter Pk. Ter.
38	A1	Baxter St.
38	B2	Bell St.
38	C1	Bellefield Av.
38	B1	Bellfield St.
38	A1	Benvie Rd.
38	B1	Black St.
38	B1	Blackness St.
38	B1	Blackscroft
39	A3	Blaikies Ms.
		Alexander St.
38	B2	Blinshall St.
38	A1	Blyth Pl.
38	B1	Blyth St.
38	B2	Bonnethill Ct.
		Hilltown Ter.
39	A3	Bonnybank Rd.
38	B1	Brewery La.
38	B1	Brook St.
39	A3	Brougham Gdns.
39	B4	Broughty Ferry Rd.
38	B3	Brown Constable St.
38	B2	Brown St.
38	A2	Bruce St.
39	A4	Buchanan St.
38	A2	Bucklemaker Ct.
		Harcourt St.
38	A2	Burgess St.
38	A2	Butterburn Sq.

C

39	A3	Caldrum St.
39	A3	Caldrum Ter.
39	B3	Callender Gdns.
38	A1	Campbell St.
39	B3	Camperdown St.
39	B3	Candle La.
39	A4	Cardean St.
38	A2	Carmichael St.
39	A3	Carnegie Sq.
		Ann St.
39	A3	Carnegie St.
39	A3	Carnegie Twr.
		Alexander St.
39	B3	Castle St.
39	A4	Catherine St.
39	A4	Chalmers St.
38	B2	Chapel St.
		Meadowside

39	A3	Church St.
38	A1	City Rd.
38	B3	City Sq.
38	A1	Cleghorn St.
39	A3	Clepington St.
39	A4	Clive St.
38	A1	Cobden St.
38	A1	Commercial St.
39	B3	Constable St.
38	B2	Constitution Rd.
38	A2	Constitution St.
38	A2	Constitution Ter.
38	B1	Corso St.
38	A3	Cotton Rd.
38	A3	Court St.
39	A4	Court St. N.
38	C2	Courthouse Sq.
38	C2	Coutties Wynd
39	A3	Cowan St.
39	B3	Cowgate
39	B4	Craigie St.
39	B3	Crescent La.
39	B3	Crescent St.
38	B2	Crichton St.
38	B2	Cross La.
38	B2	Cross Row
39	B3	Cunningham St.

D

38	B2	Dalfield St.
		Hilltown Ter.
38	B1	Daniel St.
39	B3	Dens Brae
39	A3	Dens Rd.
39	B3	Dens St.
39	A4	Derby St.
38	C2	Discovery Quay
38	A3	Dock St.
38	A2	Dons Rd.
38	B1	Douglas St.
38	A2	Douglas Ter.
38	A2	Drummond St.
38	A1	Dudhope Ct.
38	B2	Dudhope Cres. Rd.
38	B2	Dudhope St.
38	A1	Dudhope Ter.
39	A4	Duff St.
38	A2	Dunblane Pl.
39	A3	Dundonald St.
39	A3	Dura St.
39	A3	Dykehead Pl.

E

39	B3	Eadies Rd.
39	C3	Earl Grey Pl.
38	B1	Eassons Angle
39	B3	East Dock St.
38	B2	East Hendersons Wynd
39	B3	East Marketgait
38	A2	East Somerville Pl.
38	B3	East Whale La.
39	B4	Eden St.
39	B4	Eden Ter.
38	B1	Edward St.
39	A4	Eliza St.
39	A3	Ellen St.
39	B4	Ellengowan Dr.
39	B4	Erskine St.
38	B2	Euclid Cres.
38	B2	Euclid St.
39	B3	Exchange St.

F

39	A3	Fairbairn St.
39	B4	Ferguson St.
38	A2	Fingask St.
38	B1	Fleuchar St.
38	B1	Fords La.
		Perth Rd.
39	B3	Forebank Rd.
39	B3	Forebank St.
		Forebank Rd.
39	B3	Forebank Ter.
		Forebank Rd.
38	B1	Forest Pk. Pl.
38	B1	Forest Pk. Rd.
38	B2	Forester St.
39	A4	Forfar Rd.

39	B3	Foundry La.
38	A2	Fraser St.
38	A1	Fullarton St.
38	B1	Fyffe St.

G

38	B1	Gardners La.
38	B2	Garland Pl.
38	B3	Gellatly St.
39	A4	Gibson Ter.
39	A3	Glamis St.
38	B1	Glenagnes Rd.
38	A1	Gordon St.
38	B1	Gowrie St.
38	B2	Graham Pl.
38	C1	Greenfield Pl.
38	C2	Greenmarket
38	B2	Guthrie St.

H

38	A2	Harcourt St.
39	A4	Harriet St.
38	B1	Hawkhill
38	B1	Hawkhill Pl.
38	B1	Hawkhill W.
38	B2	Heathfield Pl.
		Old Hawkhill
38	B2	High St.
38	A2	Hill Sq.
38	A2	Hill St.
38	A3	Hillbank Gdns.
39	A3	Hillbank Pl.
		Hillbank Rd.
39	A3	Hillbank Rd.
39	A3	Hilltown
38	B2	Hilltown Ct.
		Hilltown Ter.
38	B2	Hilltown Ter.
38	B1	Hop St.
39	B3	Horse Wynd
38	B2	Horsewater Wynd
38	B2	Hunter St.

I

38	A1	Inverary Ter.
38	A1	Inverlaw Pl.
38	A1	Inverlaw Steps
38	A3	Isla St.

J

39	A3	Jamaica Sq.
		Ann St.
39	A3	Jamaica St.
39	A3	Jamaica Twr.
		Alexander St.
39	A3	James St.
39	A4	Janefield Pl.
38	B2	Johnston St.

K

38	A2	Keats Pl.
39	B4	Kemback St.
38	A1	Kenmore Ter.
38	A2	Kennet Wk.
38	A1	Killin Av.
39	A3	Kincaldrum Pl.
38	B1	Kincardine St.
39	B3	King St.
38	A2	Kinghorne Ct.
		Kinghorne Rd.
38	A2	Kinghorne Pl.
		Kinghorne Rd.
38	A1	Kinghorne Rd.
38	A2	Kinghorne Ter.
38	A2	Kinghorne Wk.
38	A2	Kinloch St.
38	A2	Kinloch Ter.
		Stirling Av.
38	A2	Kinnaird St.
39	B3	Kirk La.
38	C2	Kirk Style
		Nethergate

L

38	B2	Laburn St.
		Dudhope Cres. Rd.
38	A2	Ladywell Av.
39	A3	Laing Pl.
		Laing St.

39	A3	Laing St.
39	A3	Lambs La.
39	A4	Langlands St.
38	B1	Larch St.
38	B2	Laurel Bk.
38	A1	Law Cres.
38	A2	Law Rd.
38	A2	Law St.
38	B1	Lawrence St.
38	A1	Lawside Av.
38	A1	Lawside Rd.
38	A1	Lawside Ter.
38	A2	Lawson Pl.
38	A2	Leng St.
39	B4	Lilybank Rd.
39	B4	Lilybank Ter.
38	A1	Lochee Rd.
38	B1	Lower Pleasance
39	A4	Lynnewood Pl.
38	B3	Lyon St.
38	B1	Lytton St.

M

38	A2	Macaulay St.
39	A4	Madeira St.
38	C1	Magdalen Pl.
38	A3	Main St.
39	A4	Mains Ln.
39	A3	Mains Rd.
38	A4	Maitland St.
39	A4	Malcolm St.
38	B2	Malcolms Penn
38	C3	Marine Par.
38	B4	Market St.
38	B2	Marketgait
39	B3	Martingale Gdns.
		Victoria Rd.
39	B3	Mary Slessor Sq.
39	B3	Maryann La.
39	A4	Maryfield Ter.
39	A3	Maxwelltown Twr.
		Alexander St.
38	B2	McDonald St.
39	A4	McGill St.
38	C1	McGonagall Sq.
		Patons La.
38	A2	McKinnon St.
38	C1	McVicars La.
39	B3	Meadow Entry
		Commercial St.
39	B3	Meadow La.
39	B3	Meadow Pl. Bldgs.
		Victoria Rd.
38	A2	Meadowside
39	A4	Melrose Ter.
38	B4	Melville La.
39	A3	Mid Rd.
38	B2	Mid St.
38	B1	Mid Wynd
38	B3	Middle St.
38	B1	Millers Wynd
38	B2	Miln St.
38	B1	Milnbank Rd.
38	B1	Milnes E. Wynd
38	A2	Minard Cres.
38	A1	Mitchell St.
38	A4	Molison St.
38	B4	Morgan Pl.
38	B4	Morgan St.
38	A2	Mortimer St.
39	B3	Murraygate

N

39	A3	Neish St.
39	A3	Nelson St.
39	A3	Nelson Ter.
		Nelson St.
38	C2	Nethergate
38	B2	New Inn Entry
		High St.
38	B2	Nicoll St.
39	A3	North Ellen St.
39	A4	North Erskine St.
39	A3	North George St.
39	A3	North Isla St.
38	B2	North Lindsay St.
38	A2	North Marketgait
38	A2	North Somerville Pl.
38	A2	North St.

39	A3	North Wellington St.
39	A3	North William St.

O

39	A3	Ogilvie St.
38	A2	Ogilvie's Rd.
38	B1	Old Hawkhill
38	B2	Overgate La.

P

38	C2	Palais Ct.
38	B2	Panmure St.
38	A2	Panmure Ter.
38	B2	Paradise Rd.
39	A4	Park Av.
38	B2	Park Pl.
38	B1	Park St.
38	B2	Park Wynd
38	B2	Parker St.
38	C1	Patons La.
38	B1	Peddie St.
39	B4	Peep O'day La.
38	B1	Pennycook La.
38	A1	Perth Rd.
39	B3	Peter St.
38	A1	Pitfour St.
39	A4	Pitkerro Rd.
38	A1	Pole St.
38	B1	Polepark Rd.
39	A3	Powrie Pl.
39	B3	Princes St.
38	B2	Prospect St.

Q

39	B3	Queen St.

R

39	B4	Raglan St.
38	A1	Rankine St.
38	B2	Rattray St.
38	A2	Reform St.
38	A2	Reid Sq.
		Reid St.
38	A2	Reid St.
38	B1	Ritchie's La.
38	C1	Riverside App.
39	B4	Robertson St.
39	B4	Roodyards Rd.
38	C1	Roseangle
38	A2	Rosebank Pl.
38	A2	Rosebank Rd.
38	A2	Rosebank St.
38	A1	Rosebery St.
38	B1	Rosefield St.
38	A2	Rosemount Ter.
		UpperConstitutionSt.
39	B3	Royal Ex. Ct.
		Albert Sq.
38	B2	Royal Ex. La.
		Meadowside
38	A2	Russell Pl.
38	B1	Ryehill La.

S

39	B3	St. Andrews La.
		St. Andrews St.
39	B3	St. Andrews St.
38	B2	St. Davids La.
		Marketgait
38	A1	St. Mary Pl.
38	A1	St. Mary St.
39	B4	St. Matthews La.
38	B1	St. Peter St.
39	B3	St. Roques La.
39	A3	St. Salvador St.
38	A2	Salem St.
		Constitution Rd.
38	C2	Seabraes
38	C2	Seabraes La.
38	C1	Seafield Clo.
38	C1	Seafield La.
38	C1	Seafield Rd.
39	B3	Seagate
38	B2	Session St.
39	A4	Shamrock St.
38	A1	Shelley Gdns.
39	C3	Shore Ter.
		Castle St.

39	A3	Sibbald St.
38	B2	Smalls La.
38	B2	Smalls Wynd
38	B2	Smellies La.
		Lochee Rd.
38	B2	Soap Wks. La.
38	A2	Somerville Pl.
39	B4	South Baffin St.
39	B3	South George St.
39	C3	South Marketgait
38	B2	South Tay St.
38	B2	South Ward Rd.
38	C1	Spinners Wynd
		Taylors La.
38	C1	Springfield
39	B4	Springhill
39	B4	Springhill Gdns.
38	C1	Step Row
38	A2	Stirling Av.
38	A2	Stirling St.
38	A2	Stirling Ter.
		Stirling Av.

39	A4	Stobswell Rd.
39	A3	Strathmore St.
39	B3	Sugarhouse Wynd

T

38	B1	Taits La.
39	A3	Tannadice St.
38	C2	Tay Sq.
38	C2	Tay St. La.
		Nethergate
38	C1	Tayfield Pl.
		Patons La.
38	C1	Taylors La.
38	B2	Temple La.
39	A3	Thistle St.
38	C1	Thomson St.
39	B4	Thornbank Pk.
39	B4	Thornbank St.
39	B4	Thornbank Ter.
39	B3	Trades La.
38	A1	Tullideph Pl.
38	A1	Tullideph St.

38	B2	Tulloch Ct.
		Hilltown Ter.
38	B2	Tulloch Cres.

U

38	C1	Union Pl.
38	C2	Union St.
38	B2	Union Ter.
38	A2	UpperConstitutionSt.
38	B1	Ure St.
38	B1	Urquhart St.

V

39	B3	Victoria Rd.
39	B3	Victoria St.

W

39	A3	Walker's Mill
39	B4	Wallace St.
39	A4	Walrond St.
38	B1	Walton St.
38	B2	Ward Rd.

39	B4	Watson St.
38	B1	Watsons La.
		Hawkhill
39	B3	Weavers Yd.
38	B1	Well Rd.
39	B3	Wellgate Cen.
39	A3	Wellington Sq.
		Ann St.
39	B3	Wellington St.
39	A3	Wellington Twr.
		Alexander St.
38	B2	West Bell St.
38	B2	West Hendersons Wynd
39	B3	West Lyon St.
38	A2	West Marketgait
38	B2	West Port
38	A2	West Somerville Pl.
38	B1	West Wynd
38	C1	Westfield Av.
38	C1	Westfield La.
38	C1	Westfield Pl.

38	B2	Whitehall Cres.
38	B2	Whitehall St.
39	A4	Whortley Pl.
38	B1	Wilkies La.
39	B3	William Barclay Sq.
39	A3	William St.
38	B2	Willison St.
38	A2	Wishart St.
		Stirling Av.
39	A3	Wolseley St.
39	A4	Wortley Pl.

Y

38	C2	Yeaman Shore
		Union St.

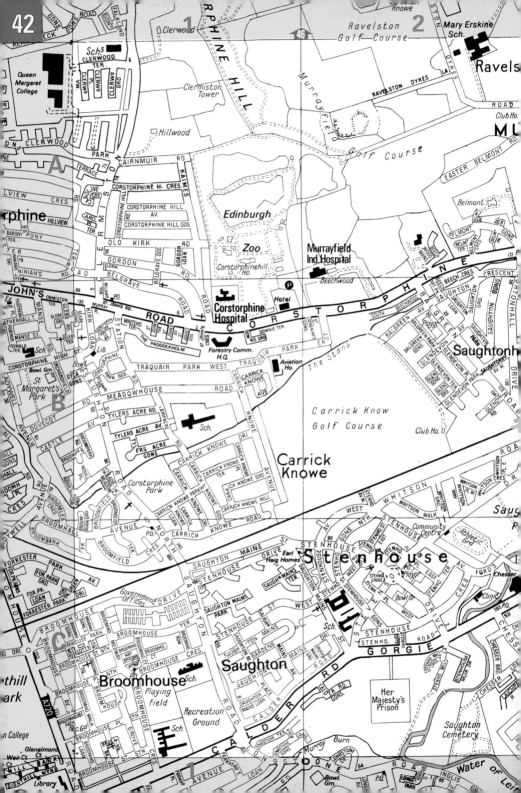

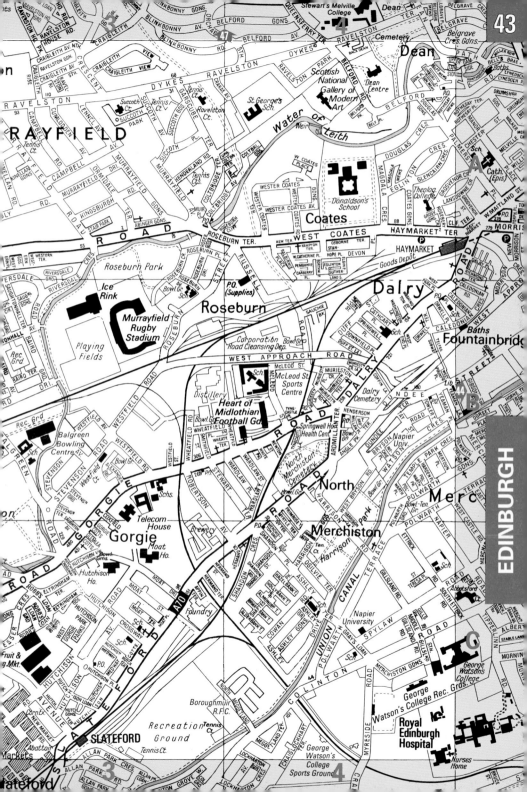

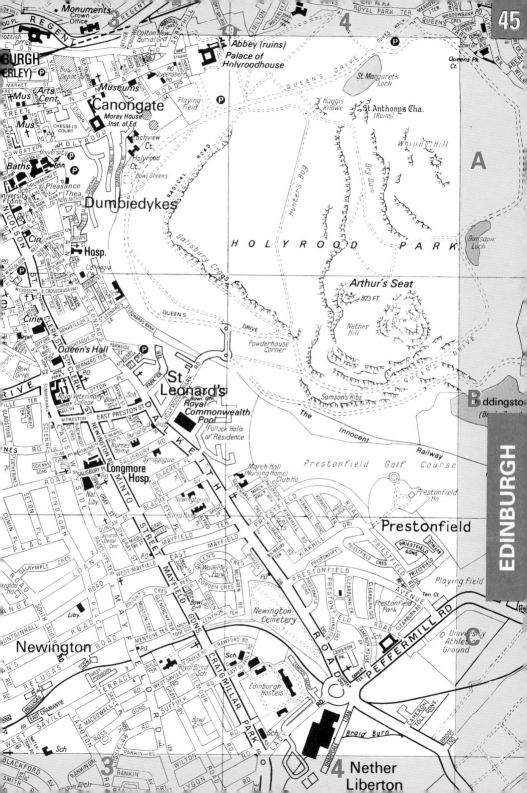

EDINBURGH

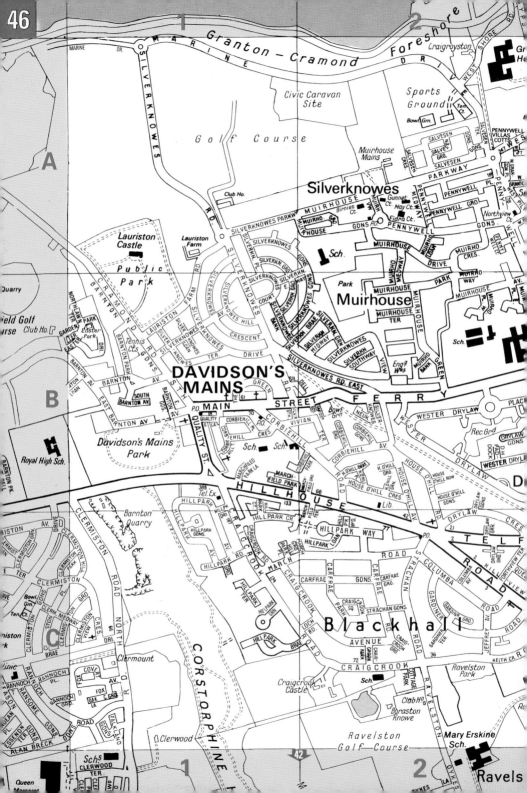

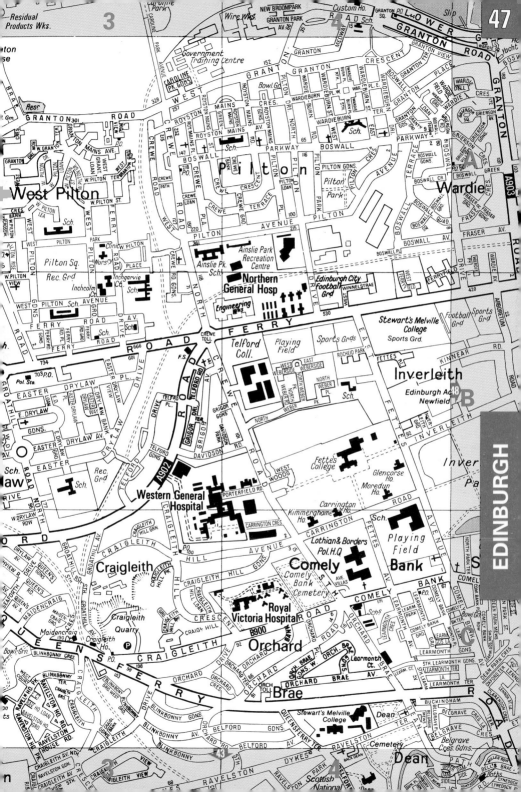

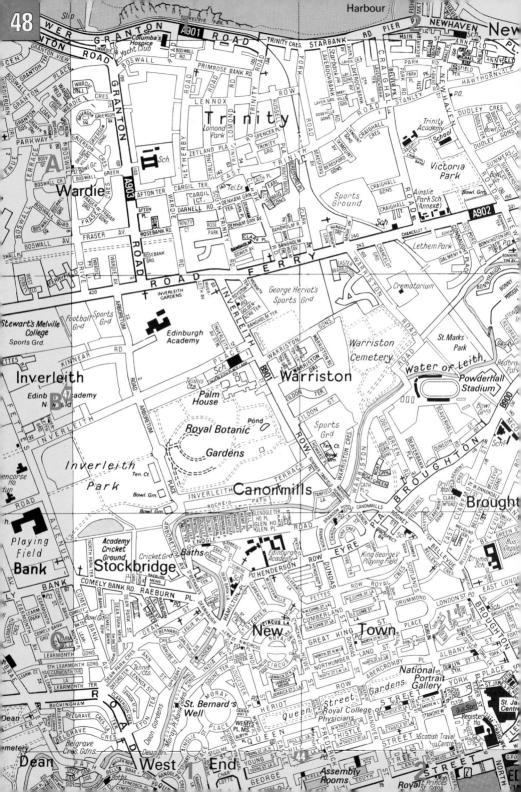

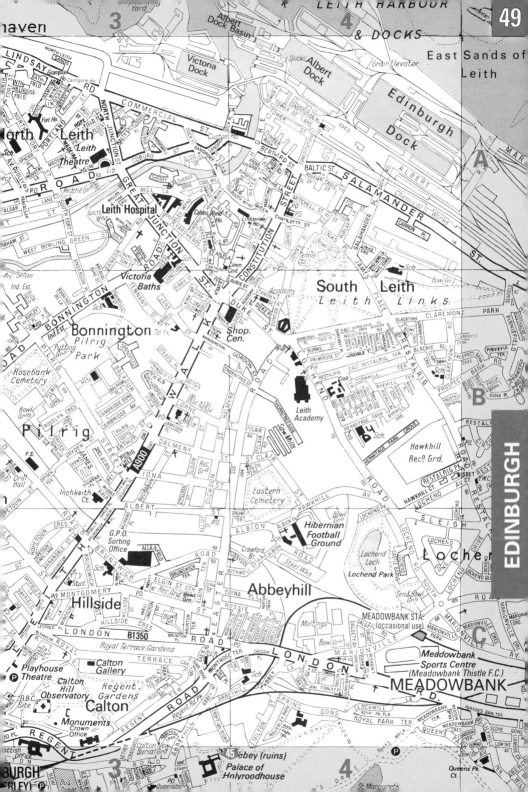

INDEX TO STREET NAMES

A

49 C3 Abbeyhill Cres.
49 C4 Abbey La.
49 C3 Abbey Mt.
45 A3 Abbey Strand
49 C4 Abbey St.
44 C1 Abbotsford Ct.
44 C1 Abbotsford Cres.
44 C1 Abbotsford Pk.
48 C2 Abercromby Pl.
43 A3 Abinger Gdns.
49 B4 Academy St.
44 B1 Admiral Ter.
49 A3 Admiralty St.
48 A1 Afton Pl.
48 A1 Afton Ter.
48 A2 Agnew Ter.
48 C1 Ainslie Pl.
48 C2 Airlie Pl.
    Brandon St.
42 C2 Aitkenhill
48 C2 Albany La.
48 C2 Albany St.
49 C3 Albert Pl.
49 A4 Albert Rd.
49 C3 Albert St.
44 C1 Albert Ter.
49 C4 Albion Pl.
49 C4 Albion Rd.
49 C4 Albion Ter.
48 C1 Albyn Pl.
43 C4 Alderbank Gdns.
    Alderbank Ter.
43 C4 Alderbank Pl.
    Alderbank Ter.
43 C4 Alderbank Ter.
43 B3 Alexander Dr.
45 C3 Alfred Pl.
43 C3 Allan Park Cres.
43 C4 Almondbank Ter.
44 B1 Alvanley Ter.
    Whitehouse Loan
49 C4 Alva Pl.
44 A1 Alva St.
49 B3 Anderson Pl.
43 B4 Angle Park Ter.
49 C3 Annandale St. La.
48 C2 Annandale St.
49 A3 Annfield
48 A2 Annfield St.
48 C1 Ann St.
49 C3 Antigua St.
42 B1 Anworth Vill.
    Saughton Rd. N.
43 C3 Appin Ter.
48 C1 Arboretum Av.
48 B1 Arboretum Rd.
44 A2 Archibald Pl.
44 B2 Arden St.
43 B4 Ardmillan Pl.
43 B4 Ardmillan Ter.
43 B4 Ardmillan Terrace La.
    Ardmillan Ter.
44 B2 Argyle Park Ter.
44 B2 Argyle Pl.
43 A3 Argyle St.
44 A1 Argyll Ter.
    Dalry Pl.
45 A3 Arthur Pl.
    Arthur St.
49 B3 Arthur St.
45 A3 Arthur St.
44 C2 Ashfield
43 C4 Ashley Dr.
43 C4 Ashley Gdns.
43 C4 Ashley Gro.
43 B3 Ashley Pl.
43 C4 Ashley Ter.
49 B4 Ashville Ter.
49 A4 Assembly St.
44 A1 Atholl Cres.
44 A1 Atholl Pl.
    West Maitland St.
44 A1 Atholl Ter.
    Dalry Pl.
48 A2 Auchinleck Ct.
48 C1 Avondale Pl.

B

43 A4 Back Dean
43 B3 Baird Av.
43 B3 Baird Dr.
43 B3 Baird Gdns.
43 B3 Baird Gro.
43 B3 Baird Ter.
48 C1 Bakers Pl.
    Kerr St.
43 A4 Balbirnie Pl.
49 B3 Balfour Pl.
49 B3 Balfour St.
42 B2 Balgreen Av.
42 B2 Balgreen Gdns.
42 B2 Balgreen Pk.
42 B2 Balgreen Rd.
49 A3 Ballantyne Lane
    Ballantyne Rd.
49 A3 Ballantyne Pl.
    Ballantyne Rd.
49 A3 Ballantyne Rd.
48 C1 Balmoral Pl.
44 A4 Baltic St.
48 A1 Bangholm Av.
48 A1 Bangholm Bower Av.
48 A2 Bangholm Gro.
48 A1 Bangholm Loan
48 A1 Bangholm Pk.
48 A1 Bangholm Pl.
48 A1 Bangholm Rd.
48 B1 Bangholm Ter.
48 A2 Bangholm Vw.
48 A2 Bangholm Vill.
    Ferry Rd.
49 A3 Bangor Rd.
44 A2 Bank St.
44 B1 Barclay Pl.
    Bruntsfield Pl.
44 B1 Barclay Ter.
46 B1 Barnton Av. E.
46 B1 Barnton Av. S.
46 B1 Barnton Gdns.
46 B1 Barnton Loan
46 B1 Barnton Pk.
48 C2 Barony Pl.
48 C2 Barony St.
49 A3 Bathfield Rd.
49 A4 Bath Rd.
45 A3 Baxters Bldgs.
    Holyrood Rd.
49 C3 Baxters Pl.
    Leith Wk.
44 C2 Beaufort Rd.
48 B2 Beaverbank Pl.
48 B2 Beaverhall Rd.
48 C1 Bedford Ct.
48 C1 Bedford St.
42 A2 Beechmount Cres.
42 A2 Beechmount Park
49 B4 Beechwood Ter.
47 C4 Belford Av.
43 A4 Belford Bridge
    Belford Rd.
47 C4 Belford Gdns.
43 A4 Belford Mews
43 A4 Belford Pk.
43 A4 Belford Pl.
43 A4 Belford Rd.
43 A4 Belford Ter.
    Belford Rd.
47 C4 Belgrave Cres.
47 C1 Belgrave Crescent La.
42 A1 Belgrave Gdns.
47 C4 Belgrave Mews
47 C4 Belgrave Pl.
42 A1 Belgrave Rd.
42 B1 Belgrave Ter.
48 C2 Bellevue
48 B2 Bellevue Cres.
48 B2 Bellevue Gdns.
48 C2 Bellevue La.
48 C2 Bellevue Gro.
48 C2 Bellevue Pl.
48 C2 Bellevue Rd.
48 C2 Bellevue St.
48 C2 Bellevue Ter.
48 C1 Bell Pl.
44 A1 Bells Brae
44 A1 Bells Wynd
    High St.

42 A2 Belmont Av.
42 A2 Belmont Cres.
42 A2 Belmont Gdns.
42 A2 Belmont Pk.
42 A2 Belmont Ter.
42 A2 Belmont Vw.
48 A2 Belvedere Pk.
48 A2 Beresford Av.
42 A2 Beresford Gdns.
48 A1 Beresford Pl.
48 A2 Beresford Ter.
    Trinity Rd.
49 A4 Bernard St.
48 B3 Bernard Ter.
46 A2 Birnies Ct.
45 B3 Blacket Av.
45 B3 Blacket Pl.
45 C3 Blackford Bank
44 C2 Blackford Av.
44 C2 Blackford House
44 C2 Blackford Rd.
45 A3 Blackfriars St.
49 B4 Blackie Rd.
45 B3 Blackwood Cres.
44 A2 Blair St.
42 A2 Blantyre Ter.
49 C3 Blenheim Pl.
47 C3 Blinkbonny Av.
47 C3 Blinkbonny Gdns.
47 C3 Blinkbonny Gro.
47 C3 Blinkbonny Gro. W.
43 A3 Blinkbonny Rd.
47 C3 Blinkbonny Ter.
48 B2 Boat Grn.
48 A2 Bonar Pl.
    Ferry Rd.
48 A2 Bonnington Av.
48 A2 Bonnington Gro.
49 B3 Bonnington Rd.
49 B3 Bonnington Road La.
48 A2 Bonnington Ter.
45 B3 Boroughloch Bldgs.
    Boroughloch Sq.
45 B3 Boroughloch Sq.
45 B3 Boroughloch La.
44 A2 Borthwick Clo.
    High St.
43 A4 Borthwick Pl.
47 A4 Boswall Av.
47 A4 Boswall Cres.
47 A4 Boswall Dr.
47 A4 Boswall Gdns.
48 A1 Boswall Grn.
47 A4 Boswall Gro.
47 A4 Boswall Loan
47 A4 Boswall Parkway
47 A4 Boswall Pl.
44 A4 Boswall Quadrant
48 A1 Boswall Rd.
47 A4 Boswall Sq.
47 A4 Boswall Ter.
49 C4 Bothwell St.
48 B1 Bowhill Ter.
    Ferry Rd.
49 A4 Bowies Clo.
    Queen St.
49 A3 Bowling Green St.
49 A3 Bowling Green St. W.
    Bowling Green St.
45 B3 Bowmont Pl.
45 A3 Boyds Entry
    St. Marys St.
44 B1 Brandfield St.
48 C2 Brandon St.
48 C2 Brandon Ter.
49 C3 Brand Pl.
    Abbeyhill
42 C2 Breadalbane St.
48 A1 Breadalbane Ter.
    Dalry Pl.
44 A1 Bread St.
49 A3 Brewery La.
    Great Junction St.
43 C4 Briarbank Ter.
49 A3 Brickwork Clo.
    Giles St.
45 C4 Bridge End

48 C1 Bridge Pl.
    Glenogle Rd.
45 A3 Briery Bauks
44 A2 Brighton St.
45 C3 Brights Cres.
44 A1 Bright Ter.
    Dairy Pl.
44 A2 Bristo Pl.
44 A2 Bristo Port
49 A4 Broad Wynd
42 C1 Broomburn Gro.
42 C1 Broomfield Cres.
42 C1 Broomhouse Bank
42 C1 Broomhouse Cotts.
49 A3 Broomhouse Cotts. E.
42 C1 Broomhouse Ct.
42 C1 Broomhouse Cres.
42 C1 Broomhouse Gdns. E.
42 C1 Broomhouse Gro.
42 C1 Broomhouse Loan
42 C1 Broomhouse Medway
42 C1 Broomhouse Pl. S.
42 C1 Broomhouse Row
42 C1 Broomhouse Sq.
42 C1 Broomhouse Ter.
42 C1 Broomhouse Wk.
42 C1 Broomhouse Way
42 C1 Broomhouse Wynd
42 B1 Broompark Rd.
42 B1 Broomside Ter.
44 B2 Brougham Pl.
44 B1 Brougham St.
48 C2 Broughton Market
48 C2 Broughton Pl.
48 C2 Broughton Pl. E.
    Broughton Pl.
48 B2 Broughton Rd.
48 C2 Broughton Street La.
48 C2 Broughton St.
45 A3 Browns Clo.
44 A2 Browns Pl.
    Vennel
45 A3 Brown St.
49 C3 Brunswick Pl.
49 C3 Brunswick Rd.
49 C3 Brunswick Ter.
49 C3 Brunton Gdns.
    Montgomery St.
49 C3 Brunton Pl.
49 C3 Brunton Ter.
44 B1 Bruntsfield Av.
44 B1 Bruntsfield Cres.
44 B1 Bruntsfield Gdns.
44 B1 Bruntsfield Pl.
44 B1 Bruntsfield Ter.
43 B4 Bryson Rd.
44 B2 Buccleuch Pl.
45 B3 Buccleuch St.
45 B3 Buccleuch Ter.
49 B3 Buchanan St.
47 C4 Buckingham Ter.
49 A4 Burgess St.
45 C4 Burgess Ter.
49 A3 Burlington St.
49 B4 Burns St.

C

49 A3 Cables Wynd
49 A3 Cables Wynd Ho.
49 A4 Cadiz St.
49 C4 Cadzow Pl.
49 A3 Cairngorm Ho.
42 A1 Cairnmuir Rd.
48 A1 Caithness Pl.
42 C2 Calder Road Gdns.
43 B4 Caledonian Cres.
43 B4 Caledonian Pl.
44 B1 Caledonian Rd.
49 C3 Calton Hill
45 A3 Calton Rd.
49 B3 Cambridge Av.
49 B3 Cambridge Gdns.
44 A1 Cambridge Street La.
44 A1 Cambridge St.
45 C4 Cameron Cres.

45 C4 Cameron House Av.
45 C4 Cameron Pk.
45 C4 Cameron Ter.
45 C4 Cameron Toll Gdns.
43 A3 Campbell Av.
43 A3 Campbell Rd.
45 A3 Campbells Clo.
49 C4 Cambusnethan St.
44 C1 Canaan La.
44 A2 Candlemaker Row
44 A1 Canning Street La.
44 A1 Canning St.
48 C2 Cannon La. .
49 A3 Cannon Wynd
45 A3 Canongate
48 B2 Canonmills
48 C2 Canon St.
43 A4 Carberry Pl.
46 C2 Carfrae Gdns.
46 C2 Carfrae Gro.
46 C2 Carfrae Pk.
46 C2 Carfrae Rd.
48 A1 Cargil Ct.
48 A1 Cargil Ter.
48 C1 Carlton St.
49 C3 Carlton Ter.
49 C4 Carlyle Pl.
45 A3 Carnegie Ct.
45 A3 Carnegie St.
42 A1 Caroline Gdns.
47 A3 Caroline Park Av.
42 A1 Caroline Pl.
49 A4 Carpet La.
42 B1 Carrick Knowe Av.
42 B1 Carrick Knowe Dr.
42 B1 Carrick Knowe Gdns.
42 B1 Carrick Knowe Gro.
42 B1 Carrick Knowe Hill
42 B1 Carrick Knowe Loan
42 B1 Carrick Knowe Parkway
42 B1 Carrick Knowe Pl.
42 C1 Carrick Knowe Rd.
42 B1 Carrick Knowe Ter.
47 C4 Carrington Rd.
44 A2 Carrubbers Clo.
    High St.
49 B3 Casselbank St.
49 B3 Cassels La.
44 A2 Castle Esplanade
44 A1 Castlehill
44 A1 Castle St.
44 A1 Castle Ter.
44 A2 Castle Wynd N.
    Johnston Ter.
44 A2 Castle Wynd S.
    Johnston Ter.
43 B4 Cathcart Pl.
48 C2 Cathedral La.
45 B3 Causewayside
44 B1 Chalmers Bldgs.
    Fountainbridge
45 A3 Chalmers Clo.
44 B2 Chalmers Cres.
44 B2 Chalmers St.
44 C1 Chamberlain Rd.
44 A2 Chambers St.
48 A2 Chancelot Cres.
    Ferry Rd.
48 A2 Chancelot Gro.
48 A2 Chancelot Ter.
49 A4 Chapel La.
45 B3 Chapel St.
44 A2 Charlesfield
    Bristo Sq.
44 A2 Charles Street La.
    George Sq.
44 A1 Charlotte La.
44 A1 Charlotte Sq.
49 C3 Charlton Terrace La.
44 C2 Charterhall Gro.
42 C2 Chesser Av.
43 C3 Chesser Cres.
42 C2 Chesser Gdns.
42 C2 Chesser Gro.
42 C2 Chesser Loan
45 A3 Chessels
44 A1 Chester St.
48 C1 Cheyne St.

44 C1 Church Hill
44 C1 Churchill Dri.
44 C1 Church Hill Pl.
48 C1 Circus Gdns.
48 C1 Circus La.
49 A3 Citadel St.
Commercial St.
49 A3 Citadel Pl.
49 C4 Clapperton Pl.
Lower London Rd.
49 B4 Clarebank Cres.
48 C2 Claremont Bank
48 B2 Claremont Cres.
49 B4 Claremont Gdns.
48 B2 Claremont Gro.
49 B4 Claremont Pk.
49 B4 Claremont Rd.
48 C1 Clarence St.
48 C1 Clarendon Cres.
48 A2 Clark Av.
48 A1 Clark Pl.
48 A1 Clark Rd.
45 C4 Clearburn Cres.
45 C4 Clearburn Gdns.
45 C4 Clearburn Rd.
45 B3 Clerk St.
46 C1 Clermiston Hill
42 A1 Clermiston Rd.
46 C1 Clermiston Rd. N.
42 A1 Clermiston Ter.
46 C1 Clermiston Vw.
42 A1 Clerwood Gro.
42 A1 Clerwood Pl.
42 A1 Clerwood Ter.
42 A1 Clerwood Vw.
43 A4 Clifton Ter.
44 C1 Clinton Rd.
49 C4 Clockmill La.
42 C2 Cluny Pl.
48 C2 Clyde St.
49 A3 Coal Hill
44 A1 Coates Cres.
43 A4 Coates Gdns.
44 A1 Coates Pl.
West Maitland St.
49 A4 Coatfield La.
45 C3 Cobden Cres.
45 C3 Cobden Rd.
44 A1 Cobden Ter.
Dalry Pl.
49 A3 Coburg St.
49 B4 Cochrane Pl.
48 C2 Cochran St.
East London St.
48 C2 Cochran Ter.
43 B4 Coffin La.
45 A3 Coinyie-House Clo.
Blackfriars St
44 C1 Colinton Rd.
43 C4 Colinton Rd.
44 A2 College Wynd
Cowgate
48 C1 Collins Pl.
43 A3 Coltbridge Av.
43 A4 Coltbridge Gdns.
43 A3 Coltbridge Ter.
43 A4 Coltbridge Vale
46 C2 Columba Av.
46 C2 Columba Rd.
48 C1 Colville Pl.
47 C4 Comely Bank
48 C1 Comely Bank Av.
47 C4 Comely Bank Gro.
48 C1 Comely Bank Pl.
48 C1 Comely Bank Place
Mews
Comely Bank Pl.
48 C1 Comely Bank Rd.
48 C1 Comely Bank Row
47 C4 Comely Bank St.
48 C1 Comely Bank Ter.
49 C4 Comely Green Cres.
49 C4 Comely Green Pl.
49 A3 Commercial St.
48 A2 Connaught Pl.
49 A4 Constitution Pl.
Tower Street La.
49 A4 Constitution St.
48 B2 Corbiehill Av.

46 B1 Corbiehill Cres.
46 B2 Corbiehill Gdns.
46 B2 Corbiehill Gro.
46 B2 Corbiehill Pk.
46 B1 Corbiehill Pl.
46 B1 Corbiehill Rd.
46 B1 Corbiehill Ter.
43 C3 Corn Exchange
Bldgs.
New Market Rd.
49 B4 Cornhill Ter.
48 C2 Cornwallis Pl.
Bellevue Cres.
44 A1 Cornwall St.
44 B2 Coronation Wk.
42 A1 Corstorphine Hill
Av.
42 A1 Corstorphine Hill
Cres.
42 A1 Corstorphine Hill
Gdns.
42 A1 Corstorphine Hill
Rd.
42 B1 Corstorphine Ho.
Av.
42 B1 Corstorphine Ho.
Ter.
42 B1 Corstorphine Park
Gdns.
42 B1 Corstorphine Rd.
49 A3 Corunna Pl.
49 A3 Couper St.
43 C4 Cowan Rd.
45 B3 Cowans Clo.
Saunders St.
44 A2 Cowgate
44 A2 Cowgatehead
46 C1 Craigcrook Av.
46 C2 Craigcrook Gdns.
46 C2 Craigcrook Pk.
46 C2 Craigcrook Pl.
Craigcrook Av.
46 C1 Craigcrook Rd.
46 C2 Craigcrook Sq.
48 A2 Craighall Av.
Craighall Av.
48 A2 Craighall Bank
48 A2 Craighall Cres.
48 A2 Craighall Gdns.
48 A2 Craighall Rd.
48 A2 Craighall Ter.
43 A3 Craigleith Av. N.
43 A3 Craigleith Av. S.
47 C3 Craigleith Bank
47 C3 Craigleith Cres.
47 C3 Craigleith Dr.
47 C3 Craigleith Gdns.
47 C3 Craigleith Gro.
47 C3 Craigleith Hill
47 C3 Craigleith Hill Av.
47 C3 Craigleith Hill Cres.
47 C3 Craigleith Hill
Gdns.
47 C3 Craigleith Hill Grn.
47 C3 Craigleith Hill Gro.
47 C3 Craigleith Hill Loan
47 C3 Craigleith Hill Pk.
47 C3 Craigleith Hill Row
47 C3 Craigleith House
43 A3 Craigleith Ri.
43 A3 Craigleith Rd.
43 A3 Craigleith Vw.
43 C4 Craiglockhart Ter.
45 C4 Craigmillar Pk.
45 A3 Cranston St.
43 A3 Crarae Av.
49 C4 Crawford Bri.
45 C4 Crawfurd Rd.
43 B3 Crescent, The,
Gorgie Rd.
47 A4 Crewe Bank
47 A4 Crewe Cres.
47 A4 Crewe Gro.
47 A3 Crewe Loan
47 A4 Crewe Path
47 A3 Crewe Pl.
47 A3 Crewe Road Gdns.
47 A3 Crewe Rd. N.
47 B4 Crewe Rd. S.
47 A3 Crewe Rd. W.
47 A4 Crewe Ter.

47 B3 Crewe Toll
44 A2 Crichton St.
49 B3 Crighton Pl.
49 C3 Croall Pl.
49 C3 Croft-an-righ
49 A3 Cromwell Pl.
Commercial St.
49 B3 Crown Pl.
49 B3 Crown St.
48 C2 Cumberland St.
45 C3 Cumin Pl.
43 A3 Cumlodden Av.
49 B3 Cunningham Pl.
Jane St.

D
43 C4 Daisy Ter.
Merchiston Gro.
49 C4 Dalgety Av.
49 C4 Dalgety Rd.
49 C4 Dalgety St.
45 B3 Dalkeith Rd.
48 A2 Dalmeny Rd.
48 A2 Dalmeny St.
45 C3 Dalrymple Cres.
44 A1 Dalry Pl.
44 A1 Dalry Rd.
49 C4 Dalziel Pl.
London Rd.
43 A4 Damside
48 C1 Danube St.
48 C1 Darlings Bldgs.
Saunders St.
48 C1 Darnaway St.
44 A1 Darnell Rd.
46 B2 Davidson Gdns.
47 B3 Davidson Pk.
47 B3 Davidson Rd.
45 A3 Davie St.
48 C1 Dean Bank La.
48 C1 Dean Bank Ter.
West Claremont St.
48 C1 Deanhaugh St.
48 C1 Dean Park Cres.
48 C1 Dean Park Mews
48 C1 Dean Park St.
47 C4 Dean Path
48 C1 Dean
48 C1 Dean Ter.
43 C3 Delhaig
48 A1 Denham Green Av.
48 A1 Denham Green Pl.
48 A1 Denham Green
Ter.
48 A2 Derby St.
43 A4 Devon Pl.
48 C1 Dewar La.
44 A1 Dewar Pl.
44 C2 Dick Pl.
44 A2 Dicksons Clo.
High St.
44 A2 Dicksons Ct.
Bristo St.
49 B3 Dickson St.
44 A1 Distillery La.
Dalry Rd.
49 A3 Dock Pl.
49 A3 Dock St.
44 B1 Dorset Pl.
43 A4 Douglas Cres.
43 A4 Douglas Gdns.
43 A4 Douglas Gardens
Mews
Belford Rd.
44 A1 Douglas Ter.
Dalry Pl.
43 A4 Doune Ter.
43 B4 Downfield Pl.
42 B1 Downie Gro.
42 B1 Downie Ter.
49 C4 Dr. Begg
47 B4 Drumdryan St.
48 C2 Drummond Pl.
45 A3 Drummond St.
49 C4 Drum Park Yard
Albion Rd.
44 A1 Drumsheugh Gdns.
44 A1 Drumsheugh Pl.
Queensferry St.

49 C4 Drum Ter.
49 B3 Dryden Gdns.
45 B3 Dryden Pl.
49 B3 Dryden St.
49 B3 Dryden Ter.
47 C3 Drylaw Av.
46 C2 Drylaw Cres.
46 B2 Drylaw Gdns.
46 C2 Drylaw Grn.
46 C2 Drylaw Gro.
46 B2 Drylaw House
Gdns.
46 B2 Drylaw House
Paddock
48 C2 Dublin Meuse
48 C2 Dublin Street La.
N.
48 C2 Dublin St.
48 A2 Dudley Av.
49 A3 Dudley Av. S.
48 A2 Dudley Bank
48 A2 Dudley Cres.
48 A2 Dudley Gdns.
48 A2 Dudley Gro.
48 A2 Dudley Ter.
43 B4 Duff Street La.
43 B4 Duff St.
48 B4 Duke Pl.
48 C2 Duke Street La.
48 B4 Duke St.
49 C4 Dukes Wk.
45 A3 Dumbiedykes Rd.
44 C2 Dun-Ard Gdns.
44 B1 Dunbar St.
44 B4 Duncan Pl.
45 C3 Duncan St.
44 B1 Dundas St.
43 B4 Dundee Pl.
43 B4 Dundee St.
43 B4 Dundee Ter.
48 C2 Dundonald St.
48 A2 Dunedin St.
44 A2 Dunlops Ct.
Grassmarket
48 C1 Dunrobin Pl.

E
44 A1 Earl Grey St.
48 A1 Earl Haig Gdns.
49 C4 Earlston Pl.
London Rd.
45 A3 East Adam St.
46 B1 East Barnton Gdns.
48 C2 East Broughton Pl.
Broughton Pl.
44 B1 East Castle Rd.
45 C3 East Chamanyie
48 C2 East Claremont St.
47 C3 East Ct.
49 A3 East Cromwell St.
45 B3 East
Crosscauseway
42 A2 Easter Belmont Rd.
47 B3 Easter Drylaw Av.
47 B3 Easter Drylaw
Bank
47 B3 Easter Drylaw Dr.
47 B3 Easter Drylaw
Gdns.
47 B3 Easter Drylaw Gro.
47 B3 Easter Drylaw
Loan
47 B3 Easter Drylaw Pl.
47 B3 Easter Drylaw Vw.
47 B3 Easter Drylaw Way
49 B4 Easter Hermitage
Restalrig Rd.
46 B1 Easter Park Dr.
49 C3 Easter Rd.
47 B4 East Fettes Av.
48 B4 Easter Hermitage Pl.
48 A1 East Lillypot
48 C2 East London St.
45 A3 East Market St.
45 C3 East Mayfield
49 C3 East Montgomery
Pl.
45 B3 East Newington Pl.

49 C3 East Norton Pl.
London Rd.
45 B3 East Preston St.
49 B4 East Restalrig Ter.
48 C2 East St. James St.
*South St. James
St.*
45 C3 East Savile Rd.
48 C1 East Silvermills La.
45 C4 East Suffolk Rd.
48 A1 East Trinity Rd.
47 B4 East Weberside
44 C1 Eden La.
44 C1 Eden Ter.
Morningside Rd.
49 C4 Edina Pl.
49 C3 Edina St.
43 A4 Eglinton Cres.
44 C2 Egypt Mews
48 B2 Eildon St.
48 B1 Eildon Ter.
49 A4 Elbe St.
48 C2 Elder St.
48 C2 Elder St. E.
43 A4 Elgin Pl.
49 C3 Elgin St. N.
49 C3 Elgin St. S.
49 C3 Elgin St.
49 B3 Elizafield
42 A2 Ellersly Rd.
49 C3 Elliot St.
49 B4 Elm Pl.
49 C3 Elm Row
49 B4 Elmwood Ter.
43 C3 Eltringham Gdns.
43 C3 Eltringham Gro.
43 C3 Eltringham Ter.
44 A1 Erskine Pl.
Shandwick Pl.
48 C1 Eton Ter.
48 C1 Ettrickdale Pl.
44 B1 Ettrick Gro.
43 C4 Ettrick Rd.
48 C2 Eyre Cres.
48 C2 Eyre Pl.
48 C2 Eyre Ter.

F
44 C1 Falcon Av.
44 C1 Falcon Ct.
44 C1 Falcon Gdns.
44 C1 Falcon Rd.
44 C1 Falcon Rd. W.
44 C1 Falkland Gdns.
47 A4 Ferryfield
48 B2 Ferry Rd.
44 B2 Ferry Road Av.
47 A3 Ferry Road Dr.
47 B3 Ferry Road Gdns.
47 B3 Ferry Road Gro.
47 B3 Ferry Road Pl.
47 B4 Fettes Ri.
48 C2 Fettes Row
44 B2 Fidra Ct.
45 C3 Findhorn Pl.
44 B2 Fingal Pl.
49 B4 Fingzies Pl.
44 A2 Fleshmarket Clo.
High St.
44 C1 Forbes Rd.
45 B3 Forbes St.
42 C2 Fords Rd.
48 C1 Forres St.
49 A4 Forrest Hill
44 A2 Forrest Rd.
49 A3 Fort Ho.
48 C2 Forth St.
47 C3 Forthview Rd.
46 C2 Forthview Ter.
49 A3 Fort Pl.
44 B1 Fountainbridge
45 C3 Fountainhall Rd.
43 B4 Fowler Ter.
46 C1 Fox Covert Av.
46 C1 Fox Covert Gro.
49 A4 Fox St.
48 A1 Fraser Av.
48 A1 Fraser Cres.

48 A1 Fraser Gdns.
48 A1 Fraser Gro.
48 C2 Frederick St.
44 B1 Freer Street Ter.
   Freer St.
44 B1 Freer St.

G
48 C1 Gabriels Rd.
46 B1 Garden Ter.
46 C2 Gardiner Gro.
46 C2 Gardiner Rd.
46 C2 Gardiner Ter.
44 A1 Gardners Cres.
49 C4 Gardner St.
   Lower London Rd.
43 A3 Garscube Ter.
49 C3 Gayfield Pl.
49 C3 Gayfield Place La.
49 C3 Gayfield Sq.
49 C3 Gayfield St.
44 A2 Generals Entry
   Bristo St.
44 B2 George Sq.
44 B2 George Square La.
44 A1 George St.
44 A2 George IV Bridge
45 A3 Gibbs Entry
   Simon Sq.
49 B3 Gibson St.
44 B1 Gibson Ter.
45 B3 Gifford Pk.
49 A3 Giles St.
44 B1 Gillespie Cres.
44 B1 Gillespie Pl.
   Leven St.
44 B1 Gillespie St.
   Gilmore Pl.
43 C4 Gillsland Pk.
43 C4 Gillsland Rd.
44 B1 Gilmore Pk.
44 B1 Gilmore Pl.
44 B1 Gilmore Place La.
45 C3 Gilmour Rd.
45 A3 Gilmour St.
49 B4 Gladstone Pl.
45 B3 Gladstone Ter.
48 C1 Glanville Pl.
   Kerr St.
42 B1 Glebe Gdns.
43 A4 Glencairn Cres.
42 B2 Glendevon Av.
42 B2 Glendevon Gdns.
42 B2 Glendevon Gro.
42 B2 Glendevon Pk.
42 B2 Glendevon Pl.
42 B2 Glendevon Rd.
42 B2 Glendevon Ter.
44 A1 Glenfinlas St.
44 B1 Glengyle Ter.
44 C2 Glenisla Gdns.
43 C3 Glenlea Cotts.
48 C1 Glenogle Ho.
   Bell Pl.
48 C1 Glenogle Pl.
   Bell Pl.
48 C1 Glenogle Rd.
48 C1 Glenogle Ter.
   Bell Pl.
49 C3 Glenorchy Pl.
   Greenside Row
45 C3 Glenorchy Ter.
44 B2 Glen St.
48 C1 Gloucester La.
48 C1 Gloucester Pl.
48 C1 Gloucester Sq.
   Gloucester La.
48 C1 Gloucester St.
49 B4 Glover St.
48 B1 Goldenacre Ter.
42 A1 Gordon Loan
42 A1 Gordon Rd.
49 B4 Gordon St.
43 C3 Gorgie Cotts.
42 C2 Gorgie Rd.
48 A2 Gosford Pl.
49 A3 Graham St.
49 A3 Grampian Ho.
45 C3 Granby Rd.

45 B3 Grange Ct.
   Causewayside
44 C2 Grange Cres.
44 C2 Grange Loan
44 C2 Grange Loan Gdns.
44 B2 Grange Rd.
44 C2 Grange Ter.
47 A4 Granton Cres.
47 A4 Granton Gdns.
47 A4 Granton Gro.
47 A3 Granton Mains Av.
47 A4 Granton Medway
47 A4 Granton Pl.
48 A1 Granton Rd.
47 A4 Granton Ter.
47 A4 Granton Vw.
45 C3 Grantully Pl.
44 B1 Granville Ter.
44 A2 Grassmarket
43 C4 Grays Loan
49 A3 Great Junction St.
48 A2 Great King St.
48 A2 Great Michael Ri.
44 A1 Great Stuart St.
44 C1 Greenhill Gdns.
44 C1 Greenhill Pk.
44 C1 Greenhill Pl.
44 B1 Greenhill Ter.
49 C3 Greenside Ct.
49 C3 Greenside La.
49 C3 Greenside Pl.
   Leith St.
49 C3 Greenside Row
48 C2 Green St.
46 B1 Green, The,
44 A2 Greyfriars Pl.
   Candlemaker Row
48 A1 Grierson Av.
48 A1 Grierson Cres.
48 A1 Grierson Gdns.
47 A4 Grierson Rd.
48 A1 Grierson Sq.
48 A1 Grierson Vill.
47 B3 Grigor Av.
47 B3 Grigor Dr.
47 B3 Grigor Gdns.
47 B3 Grigor Ter.
44 A1 Grindlay St.
44 A1 Grindlay Street Ct.
47 C3 Groathill Av.
47 C3 Groathill Gdns. E.
   Groathill Rd. S.
47 C3 Groathill Gdns. W.
   Groathill Rd. S.
47 B3 Groathill Rd. N.
47 C3 Groathill Rd. S.
43 A4 Grosvenor Cres.
43 A4 Grosvenor Gdns.
44 A1 Grosvenor St.
44 A1 Grove St.
44 A1 Grove Ter.
   Grove St.
45 A3 Gullans Clo.
   St. Marys St.
46 A2 Gunnet Ct.
44 A2 Guthrie St.

H
49 C3 Haddington Pl.
45 A3 Haddingtons Entry
   Reids Clo.
45 B3 Haddon Ct.
   Howden St.
44 B1 Hailes St.
49 A3 Halmyre St.
49 A3 Hamburgh Pl.
49 A3 Hamilton Cres.
48 C1 Hamilton Pl.
49 A3 Hamilton St.
49 A3 Hamilton Wynd
43 A4 Hampton Pl.
   West Catherine Pl.
43 A4 Hampton Ter.
48 C2 Hanover St.
43 B4 Harden Pl.
45 B3 Hardwell Clo.
48 A2 Harrison Gdns.
43 A4 Harrison La.
43 C4 Harrison Pl.
43 B4 Harrison Rd.

44 B1 Hartington Gdns.
44 B1 Hartington Pl.
48 C2 Hart St.
44 B2 Hatton Pl.
48 C1 Haugh St.
49 B4 Hawkhill Av.
49 B4 Hawkhill Ct.
49 B4 Hawkhill Vill.
   Lochend Rd.
44 A1 Hawthornbank
44 A1 Hawthornbank La.
49 A3 Hawthornbank Pl.
49 A3 Hawthornbank Ter.
   North Fort St.
44 A1 Hawthorn Bldgs.
   Belford Rd.
44 A1 Hawthorn Ter.
   Hawthornbank La.
48 A2 Hawthornvale
44 A1 Haymarket
43 A4 Haymarket Ter.
43 C4 Hazelbank Ter.
43 A3 Henderland Rd.
49 A3 Henderson Gdns.
48 C2 Henderson Pl.
48 C1 Henderson Row
49 A3 Henderson St.
43 B4 Henderson Ter.
45 B3 Henry Pl.
45 B3 Henry St.
44 A2 Heriot Bridge
44 A2 Heriot Cross
   Heriot Bridge
48 B2 Heriot Hill Ter.
44 A2 Heriot Pl.
48 C1 Heriot Row
43 C4 Hermand Cres.
43 C3 Hermand St.
43 C3 Hermand Ter.
49 B4 Hermitage Pk.
49 B4 Hermitage Park Gro.
49 B4 Hermitage Pk. S.
   Hermitage Pk.
49 B4 Hermitage Pl.
44 A1 High Riggs
45 A3 High School Yards
44 A2 High St.
46 B1 Hillhouse Rd.
46 B1 Hillpark Av.
46 B1 Hillpark Brae
46 C1 Hillpark Ct.
46 B1 Hillpark Cres.
46 B1 Hillpark Dr.
46 C1 Hillpark Gdns.
46 C1 Hillpark Gro.
46 C2 Hillpark Loan
46 C1 Hillpark Pl.
46 C1 Hillpark Rd.
46 C1 Hillpark Vw.
46 C2 Hillpark Way
46 C2 Hillpark Wood
45 A3 Hill Pl.
48 C1 Hill Street La. N.
44 A1 Hill Street La. S.
49 C3 Hillside Cres.
49 C3 Hillside St.
45 A3 Hill Sq.
   Hill Pl.
48 C1 Hill St.
46 C2 Hillview
43 C4 Hollybank Ter.
43 A3 Holyrood Ct.
45 A3 Holyrood Park Rd.
45 A3 Holyrood Rd.
44 B1 Home St.
49 A3 Hopefield Ter.
45 B3 Hope Park Cres..
44 B2 Hope Park Sq.
   Meadow La.
45 B3 Hope Park Ter.
44 A1 Hope St.
44 C2 Hope Ter.
49 C3 Hopetoun Cres.
49 C3 Hopetoun Crescent
   La.
49 B3 Hopetoun St.
44 B1 Horne Ter.
45 A3 Horse Wynd
46 B2 House O'Hill Av.

46 B2 House O'Hill Brae
46 B2 House O'Hill Cres.
46 B2 House O'Hill Gdns.
46 B2 House O'Hill Grn.
46 B2 House O'Hill Gro.
46 B2 House O'Hill Pl.
46 B2 House O'Hill Rd.
46 B2 House O'Hill Row
48 B2 Howard Pl.
48 B2 Howard St.
45 B3 Howden St.
48 C2 Howe St.
48 C1 Hugh Miller Pl.
44 A2 Hunter Sq.
48 B2 Huntly St.
43 C3 Hutchison Av.
43 C3 Hutchison Cotts.
43 C3 Hutchison Crossway
43 C3 Hutchison Gdns.
43 C3 Hutchison Gro.
43 C3 Hutchison Ho.
43 C3 Hutchison Loan
43 C3 Hutchison Medway
43 C3 Hutchison Pl.
43 C3 Hutchison Rd.
43 C3 Hutchison Ter.
43 C3 Hutchison Vw.

I
47 B3 Inchcolm Ct.
47 B3 Inchgarvie Ct.
49 B3 Inchkeith Ct.
44 A2 India Bldgs.
   Victoria St.
48 C1 India Pl.
48 C1 India St.
49 B4 Industrial Rd.
49 A3 Industry Homes
   Industry La.
49 A3 Industry La.
45 A3 Infirmary St.
44 A2 Inglis Ct.
   West Port
48 B1 Inverleith Av.
48 B1 Inverleith Av. S.
48 B1 Inverleith Gdns.
47 B4 Inverleith Gro.
47 B4 Inverleith Pl.
48 B1 Inverleith Place La.
48 B1 Inverleith Row
48 B1 Inverleith Ter.
49 B3 Iona St.
43 C4 Ivy Ter.

J
48 C1 Jamaica Mews
48 C1 Jamaica St. N. La.
48 C1 Jamaica St. S. La.
44 A2 James Ct.
   Lawnmarket
48 C2 James Craig Wk.
49 B3 Jameson Pl.
49 B3 James St.
49 B3 Jane St.
49 C4 Jane Ter.
44 B2 Jawbone Wk.
46 C2 Jeffrey Av.
45 A3 Jeffrey St.
48 A2 Jessfield Ter.
49 A3 John Russel Ct.
   Cromwell Pl.
44 A4 Johns La.
49 A4 Johns Pl.
44 A2 Johnston Ter.
44 A1 Jordan La.
49 B3 Junction Pl.

K
42 A1 Kaimes Rd.
44 A2 Keir St.
44 A2 Keith Cres.
46 C2 Keith Row
   Craigcrook Rd.
46 C2 Keith Ter.
48 C1 Kemp Pl.
48 C1 Kerr St.
43 A4 Kew Ter.

44 C2 Kilgraston Ct.
45 C4 Kilgraston Rd.
45 C4 Kilmaurs Rd.
45 C4 Kilmaurs Ter.
43 A3 Kinellan Rd.
48 A2 Kinghorn Pl.
49 A4 Kings Bridge
43 A3 Kingsburgh Rd.
44 A1 Kings Stables Rd.
44 A1 Kings Stables Road
   La.
49 A3 King St.
48 B1 Kinnear Rd.
49 A4 Kirkgate
45 C4 Kirkhill Dr.
45 B4 Kirkhill Gdns.
45 C4 Kirkhill Rd.
45 B4 Kirkhill Ter.
42 B1 Kirl Loan
49 B3 Kirk St.
49 C4 Kirkwood Pl.
   London Rd.
49 C3 Kyle Pl.

L
44 A1 Ladyfield Pl.
   Morrison St.
44 A2 Lady Lawson St.
49 C4 Lady Menzies Pl.
45 C4 Lady Rd.
44 A2 Lady Stairs Clo.
   Lawnmarket
44 A2 Lady Wynd
42 C2 Laichpark Pl.
42 C2 Laichpark Rd.
45 B3 Lambs Clo.
   East Crosscauseway
42 B1 Lampacre Rd.
45 C3 Langton Rd.
43 A4 Lansdowne Cres.
49 A3 Lapicide Pl.
49 A3 Largo Pl.
44 B2 Lauderdale St.
44 C2 Lauder Loan
44 B2 Lauder Rd.
43 B4 Laurel Ter.
   Slateford Rd.
49 B4 Laurie St.
46 B1 Lauriston Farm Rd.
44 B2 Lauriston Gdns.
44 B2 Lauriston Pk.
44 A2 Lauriston Pl.
44 A2 Lauriston St.
44 A2 Lauriston Ter.
48 A2 Laverockbank Av.
48 A2 Laverockbank Cres.
48 A2 Laverockbank Gdns.
48 A2 Laverockbank Gro.
48 A2 Laverockbank Rd.
48 A2 Laverockbank Ter.
44 A2 Lawnmarket
44 B1 Leamington Pl.
   Leamington Ter.
48 B1 Leamington Rd.
44 B1 Leamington Ter.
47 C4 Learmonth Av.
47 C4 Learmonth Ct.
47 C4 Learmonth Cres.
47 C4 Learmonth Gdns.
47 C4 Learmonth Gardens
   La.
48 C1 Learmonth Gardens
   Mews
47 C4 Learmonth Gro.
47 C4 Learmonth Pk.
48 C1 Learmonth Pl.
48 C1 Learmonth Ter.
47 C4 Learmonth Terrace
   La.
48 C2 Leith Street Ter.
   Leith St.
48 C2 Leith St.
49 C3 Leith Wk.
49 B3 Leith Wk.
43 A3 Lennel Av.
44 A1 Lennox Row
48 C1 Lennox Street La.
48 C1 Lennox St.
49 C3 Leopold Pl.

48 C1	Lelsie Pl.	
44 B1	Leven St.	
44 B2	Leven Ter.	
44 A1	Lewis Ter.	
	Dalry Pl.	
48 C2	Liddesdale Pl.	
43 C4	Lily Ter.	
44 C1	Limes, The,	
44 B4	Lindean Pl.	
44 A2	Lindsay Pl.	
	Chambers St.	
49 A3	Lindsay Pl.	
49 A3	Linsday St.	
49 B4	Links Gdns.	
49 A4	Links Gardens La.	
49 A4	Links Gro.	
49 A4	Links Pl.	
48 C4	Linkview Ho.	
48 C2	Little King St.	
44 B2	Livingstone Pl.	
48 A2	Lixmount Av.	
48 A2	Lixmount Gdns.	
49 B4	Lochend Av.	
49 C4	Lochend Castle	
	Barns	
45 A3	Lochend Clo.	
49 C4	Lochend Dr.	
49 C4	Lochend Gdns.	
49 C4	Lochend Pk.	
49 C4	Lochend Rd. S.	
49 C4	Lochend Sq.	
44 B1	Lochrin Bldgs.	
	Gilmore Pl.	
44 B1	Lochrin La.	
44 B1	Lochrin Pl.	
44 B1	Lochrin Ter.	
	Thornybank	
46 C2	Loch Rd.	
45 A3	Lochview Ct.	
43 C4	Lockharton Gdns.	
48 C2	Logan St.	
48 B2	Logie Green Gdns.	
48 B2	Logie Green Loan	
	Logie Green Rd.	
48 B2	Logie Green Rd.	
44 A1	Lomond Rd.	
49 C3	London Rd.	
48 C2	London St.	
42 C2	Longstone Cres.	
42 C1	Longstone Gdns.	
42 C1	Longstone Rd.	
42 C1	Longstone Ter.	
42 C1	Longstone Vw.	
44 B2	Lonsdale Ter.	
45 B3	Lord Russell Pl.	
	Causewayside	
49 B3	Lorne Pl.	
49 B3	Lorne Sq.	
49 B3	Lorne St.	
44 A1	Lothian Rd.	
44 A2	Lothian St.	
44 B2	Lovers Loan	
44 B1	Lower Gilmore Pl.	
49 C4	Lower London Rd.	
45 A3	Lower Viewcraig	
	Row	
	Waterston Av.	
45 B3	Lutton Pl.	
44 A1	Lynedoch Pl.	
44 A1	Lynedoch Place La.	
49 C4	Lyne St.	

M

48 B2	Macdonald Rd.	
45 C3	Macdowall Rd.	
48 C1	Mackenzie Pl.	
49 A3	Madeira Pl.	
49 A3	Madeira St.	
43 A4	Magdala Cres.	
43 A4	Magdala Mews	
47 C3	Maidencraig Ct.	
47 C3	Maidencraig Cres.	
47 C3	Maidencraig Gro.	
44 A2	Main Point	
46 B1	Main St.	
48 C1	Malta Ter.	
49 B3	Manderston St.	
44 A1	Manor Pl.	
48 C2	Mansfield Pl.	

44 B2	Mansion House	
	Rd.	
46 B2	Marchfield Gdns.	
	Hillhouse Rd.	
46 B2	Marchfield Gro.	
46 B1	Marchfield Pk.	
46 B1	Marchfield Park	
	La.	
46 C2	Marchfield Ter.	
46 C1	March Gro.	
45 B4	Marchhall Cres.	
45 B4	Marchhall Pl.	
	Marchhall Cres.	
45 B4	Marchhall Rd.	
44 B2	Marchmont Cres.	
44 B2	Marchmont Rd.	
44 B2	Marchmont St.	
46 C1	March Rd.	
44 C1	Mardale Cres.	
46 A1	Marine Dr.	
49 C4	Marionville Pk.	
49 C4	Marionville Rd.	
47 C3	Mariscihal Pl.	
	Queensferry Rd.	
49 A4	Maritime La.	
49 A4	Maritime St.	
49 C4	Market St.	
49 C4	Marshall Pl.	
	Kirkwood Pl.	
49 C3	Marshalls Ct.	
44 A2	Marshall St.	
	Nicholson Sq.	
46 A2	Martello Ct.	
49 A4	Martins Ct.	
	Bernard St.	
49 C3	Maryfield	
49 C4	Maryfield Pl.	
48 C1	Marys Pl.	
	Raeburn Pl.	
44 C1	Maxwell St.	
46 A2	May Ct.	
45 C3	Mayfield Gdns.	
45 C3	Mayfield Gardens	
	La.	
45 C3	Mayfield Rd.	
45 C3	Mayfield Ter.	
48 A2	Mayville Gdns.	
48 A2	Mayville Gdns. E.	
	South	
	Laverockbank Av.	
48 B2	McDonald Pl.	
49 B3	McDonald St.	
45 C4	McLaren Rd.	
44 A1	McLaren Ter.	
	Dalry Rd.	
43 B4	McLeod St.	
44 B1	McNeill St.	
49 C4	Meadowbank Av.	
49 C4	Meadowbank	
	Cres.	
49 C4	Meadowbank Ter.	
42 B1	Meadowhouse Rd.	
44 B2	Meadow La.	
44 B2	Meadow Pl.	
	Roseneath Ter.	
44 B2	Meadow Place La.	
	Roseneath Ter.	
43 C4	Meggetland Ter.	
44 A2	Melbourne Pl.	
	George IV Bridge	
48 C2	Melgund Ter.	
44 A1	Melville Dr.	
44 B2	Melville Dr.	
44 A1	Melville St.	
	Queensferry St.	
44 A1	Melville Street La.	
45 B3	Melville Ter.	
45 C3	Mentone Gdns.	
45 C3	Mentone Ter.	
44 A2	Merchant St.	
	Candlemaker Row	
44 B1	Merchiston Av.	
44 B1	Merchiston Bank	
	Av.	
44 C1	Merchiston Bank	
	Gdns.	
44 B1	Merchiston Cres.	
43 C4	Merchiston Gdns.	
43 C4	Merchiston Gro.	

44 B1	Merchiston Mews	
44 B1	Merchiston Pk.	
44 B1	Merchiston Pl.	
43 B4	Mertoun Pl.	
44 A2	Mouse La.	
45 C3	Middleby St.	
44 B2	Middle Meadow	
	Wk.	
49 B3	Middlesfield	
44 C1	Millar Cres.	
44 C1	Millar Pl.	
44 C1	Millar Place La.	
44 B2	Millerfield Pl.	
44 A1	Miller Row	
49 A3	Mill La.	
44 C4	Milton St.	
45 B3	Minto St.	
44 A4	Mitchell St.	
43 C3	Moat Dr.	
43 C3	Moat Ho.	
43 C3	Moat Pl.	
43 C3	Moat St.	
43 C3	Moat Ter.	
45 B3	Moncrieff Ter.	
44 C2	Monkwood Ct.	
48 B1	Monmouth Ter.	
45 B3	Montague St.	
48 B1	Montagu Ter.	
	Inverleith Row	
49 C3	Montgomery Street	
	La.	
49 C3	Montgomery St.	
44 B1	Montpelier	
44 B1	Montpelier Pk.	
44 B1	Montpelier Ter.	
49 C3	Montrose Ter.	
48 C1	Moray Pl.	
44 C1	Morningside Pk.	
44 C1	Morningside Rd.	
44 C1	Morningside Rd.	
44 C1	Morningside Ter.	
44 B1	Morrison Cres.	
44 A1	Morrison St.	
44 A1	Morrison St. Link	
44 C2	Mortonhall Rd.	
45 C3	Moston Ter.	
44 A2	Mound Pl.	
44 A2	Mound, The,	
46 B2	Muirhouse Av.	
46 B2	Muirhouse Bank	
46 A2	Muirhouse Cres.	
46 A2	Muirhouse Dr.	
46 A2	Muirhouse Gdns.	
46 B2	Muirhouse Grn.	
46 A2	Muirhouse Gro.	
46 A2	Muirhouse Loan	
46 B2	Muirhouse	
	Medway	
46 B2	Muirhouse Pk.	
46 A2	Muirhouse	
	Parkway	
46 B2	Muirhouse Pl. E.	
46 B2	Muirhouse Pl. W.	
46 A2	Muirhouse Ter.	
46 A2	Muirhouse Vw.	
46 B2	Muirhouse Way	
43 A3	Muir Pl.	
48 A2	Mulberry Pl.	
	Newhaven Rd.	
48 B2	Munro Pl.	
	Canonmills	
49 C3	Murano Pl.	
44 B1	Murdoch Ter.	
43 B4	Murieston Cres.	
43 B4	Murieston Cres.	
	La.	
43 B4	Murieston La.	
43 B4	Murieston Pl.	
43 B4	Murieston Rd.	
43 B4	Murieston Ter.	
43 A3	Murrayfield Av.	
43 A3	Murrayfield Dr.	
43 A3	Murrayfield Gdns.	
43 A3	Murrayfield Pl.	
	Coltbridge Av.	
43 A3	Murrayfield Rd.	
42 B1	Murray Pl.	
43 C4	Myreside Rd.	
43 B4	Myrtle Ter.	

N

43 C4	Napier Rd.	
48 C2	Nelson Pl.	
	Dublin Meuse	
48 C2	Nelson St.	
48 A1	Netherby Rd.	
45 A3	Nether Craigwell	
45 A3	New Arthur Pl.	
44 C1	Newbattle Ter.	
48 C2	New Broughton	
48 A2	Newhaven Rd.	
45 B3	Newington Rd.	
45 B3	New Johns Pl.	
49 A4	Newkirkgate	
	Giles St.	
48 A2	New La.	
45 C3	Newlands Pk.	
	Mayfield Gdns.	
43 C3	New Market Rd.	
42 C2	New Mart Rd.	
44 A1	New Morrison St.	
48 C1	Newport St.	
49 B3	New Orchardfield	
45 A3	New Skinners Clo.	
	Blackfriars St.	
43 B4	Newton St.	
49 A3	Nicoll Pl.	
45 A3	Nicolson Sq.	
45 A3	Nicolson St.	
44 A2	Niddry St.	
45 A3	Niddry St. S.	
	Cowgate	
44 C1	Nile Gro.	
49 B4	Nisbet Ct.	
49 B4	Noble Pl.	
44 A2	North Bank St.	
44 A2	North Bridge	
44 A1	North Charlotte St.	
48 C2	North Clyde Street La.	
43 B4	Northcote St.	
48 C1	North East Circus	
	Pl.	
48 C2	North East	
	Cumberland Street	
	La.	
48 C2	North East Thistle	
	Street La.	
49 A3	North Fort St.	
49 A3	North Junction St.	
44 A1	North La.	
46 B1	Northlawn Ter.	
49 A3	North Leith Sands	
49 A3	North Leith Mill	
44 B2	North Meadow	
	Wk.	
43 C4	North Meggetland	
48 C1	North Park Ter.	
48 C2	North St. Andrew	
	La.	
48 C2	North St. Andrew	
	St.	
48 C2	North St. David St.	
48 C2	North St. James St.	
48 C2	Northumberland	
	Pl.	
	Dublin Meuse	
48 C2	Northumberland	
	Pl. La.	
	Dublin Meuse	
48 C2	Northumberland	
	Street N.E. La.	
48 C2	Northumberland	
	Street N.W. La.	
48 C2	Northumberland	
	Street S.E. La.	
48 C2	Northumberland	
	Street S.W. La.	
48 C2	Northumberland	
	St.	
48 C2	Northumberland	
	Pl.	
	Northumberland	
	St.	
46 A2	Northview Ct.	
47 B4	North Weber Pk.	
47 B4	North Weber Pl.	
47 B4	North Weber Rd.	
48 C1	North West Circus	
	Pl.	

48 C2	North West	
	Cumberland Street	
	La.	
48 C1	North West Thistle	
	Street La.	
49 C4	Norton Pk.	
49 C3	Nottingham Ter.	
	Nottingham Pl.	

O

45 A3	Oakfield	
46 C1	Oak La.	
49 B4	Oakville Ter.	
43 C4	Ogilvie Ter.	
44 A2	Old Assembly Clo.	
	High St.	
48 C2	Old Broughton	
45 C4	Old Dalkeith Rd.	
44 A2	Old Fishmarket Clo.	
	Cowgate	
42 A1	Old Kirk Rd.	
45 A3	Old Tolbooth Wynd	
47 C4	Orchard Bank	
47 C4	Orchard Brae	
47 C4	Orchard Brae Av.	
47 C4	Orchard Brae	
	Gdns.	
47 C4	Orchard Brae	
	Gdns. W.	
47 C4	Orchard Brae W.	
	Orchard Brae	
47 C4	Orchard Cres.	
47 C3	Orchard Dr.	
49 B3	Orchardfield La.	
47 C4	Orchard Gro.	
	Orchard Rd.	
47 C4	Orchard Pl.	
47 C4	Orchard Rd.	
47 B3	Orchard Rd. S.	
47 C4	Orchard Ter.	
47 C4	Orchard Toll	
43 A3	Ormidale Ter.	
43 B4	Orwell Pl.	
43 B4	Orwell Ter.	
43 A4	Osborne Ter.	
44 C2	Oswald Ct.	
44 C2	Oswald Rd.	
45 B3	Oxford St.	
48 C1	Oxford Ter.	

P

42 B1	Paddockholm, The,	
44 A1	Palmerston Pl.	
44 A1	Palmerston Place	
	La.	
	Palmerston Pl.	
44 B2	Palmerston Rd.	
44 B2	Panmure Pl.	
48 A2	Park Pl.	
48 A2	Park Rd.	
45 B3	Parkside St.	
45 B3	Parkside Ter.	
49 B4	Parkvale Pl.	
49 A3	Parliament Pl.	
	Parliament St.	
44 A2	Parliament Sq.	
49 A3	Parliament St.	
48 C1	Patriothall	
	Hamilton Pl.	
49 A4	Pattison St.	
45 C3	Peel-Ter.	
45 C4	Peffermill Rd.	
46 B1	Peggys Pl.	
	Corbiehill Rd.	
43 A4	Pembroke Pl.	
46 A2	Pennywell Cotts.	
	West Granton Rd.	
46 A2	Pennywell Gdns.	
46 A2	Pennywell Gro.	
46 A2	Pennywell	
	Medway	
46 A2	Pennywell Rd.	
46 A2	Pennywell Rd.	
46 A2	Pennywell Vill.	
	West Granton Rd.	
48 C1	Perth St.	

48 C2 Picardy Pl.
49 B3 Pilrig Cotts.
49 B3 Pilrig Glebe
49 B3 Pilrig Gdns.
49 B3 Pilrig Pl.
   Pilrig St.
49 B3 Pilrig St.
47 A4 Pilton Av.
47 A4 Pilton Cres.
47 A4 Pilton Dr.
47 A4 Pilton Dr. N.
47 A4 Pilton Gdns.
47 A4 Pilton Loan
47 A4 Pilton Pk.
47 A4 Pilton Pl.
49 B3 Pirrie St.
49 C4 Pitlochry Pl.
   Carlyle Pl.
44 C1 Pitsligo Rd.
49 A3 Pitt St.
45 A3 Pleasance
44 B1 Polwarth Cres.
43 B4 Polwarth Gdns.
43 B4 Polwarth Gro.
43 B4 Polwarth Pk.
43 B4 Polwarth Pl.
43 C4 Polwarth Ter.
44 B1 Ponton St.
49 A4 Poplar La.
47 B4 Porterfield Rd.
48 C1 Portgower Pl.
49 A3 Portland Pl.
   Lindsay Rd.
49 A3 Portland St.
49 A3 Portland Ter.
   North Junction St.
44 A2 Portsburgh Sq.
   West Port
44 A2 Potterrow
44 A2 Potterrow Port
   Lothian St.
45 C4 Prestonfield Av.
45 C4 Prestonfield Cres.
45 C4 Prestonfield Gdns.
45 C4 Prestonfield Rd.
45 C4 Prestonfield Ter.
45 C4 Priestfield Av.
45 C4 Priestfield Cres.
45 C4 Priestfield Gdns.
45 B4 Priestfield Gro.
45 B4 Priestfield Rd.
45 B4 Priestfield Rd. N.
48 A1 Primrose Bank Rd.
44 B1 Primrose St.
43 B4 Primrose Ter.
45 A3 Prince Albert Bldgs.
   Waterston Av.
45 A3 Prince Regent St. 6
44 A1 Princes St.
48 C2 Prospect Bank
49 B4 Prospect Bank Gnds.
49 C1 Prospect Bank
49 B4 Prospect Bank Rd.

Q
46 B1 Quality Street La.
46 B1 Quality St.
45 B3 Quarry Clo.
   West
   Crosscauseway
49 A3 Quayside St.
49 A4 Queen Charlotte La.
   Queen Charlotte St.
49 A4 Queen Charlotte St.
48 C2 Queen Street Gdns.
   E.
48 C2 Queen Street Gdns.
   W.
46 C2 Queens Av.
47 C3 Queens Av. S.
45 C3 Queens Cres.
45 A4 Queens Dr.
47 C3 Queensferry Rd.
44 A1 Queensferry Street
   La.
44 A1 Queensferry St.
47 C4 Queensferry Ter.
47 C3 Queens Gdns.
49 C4 Queens Park Av.
49 C3 Queens Pl.
47 C3 Queens Rd.

48 C1 Queen St.
49 A3 Quilts Wynd

R
48 C1 Raeburn Mews
48 C1 Raeburn Pl.
48 C1 Raeburn St.
45 A3 Raes Bldgs.
   Holyrood Rd.
44 A2 Ramsay La.
44 A2 Ramsey Gdns.
44 A1 Randolph Cliff
44 A1 Randolph Cres.
44 A1 Randolph La.
44 A1 Randolph
45 B3 Rankeillor St.
45 C3 Rankin Rd.
45 C3 Ratcliffe Ter.
43 A3 Ravelston Ct.
43 A3 Ravelston Dykes
42 A2 Ravelston Dykes La.
46 C2 Ravelston Dykes
   Rd.
43 A3 Ravelston Gdns.
47 C3 Ravelston Heights
47 C3 Ravelston House
   Gro.
47 C3 Ravelston House
   Loan
47 C3 Ravelston House Pk.
47 C3 Ravelston House Rd.
43 A4 Ravelston Pk.
43 A4 Ravelston Pl.
   Belford Rd.
43 A3 Ravelston Ri.
47 C4 Ravelston Ter.
48 B2 Redbraes Gro.
48 B2 Redbraes Pl.
49 C4 Reekies Ct.
49 C4 Regent Pl.
49 C3 Regent Rd.
49 C3 Regent Ter.
49 C3 Regent Terrace
   Mews
48 C2 Register Pl.
45 A3 Reids Clo.
45 A3 Reids Ct.
48 C1 Reid Ter.
45 C3 Relugas Gdns.
45 C3 Relugas Pl.
45 C3 Relugas Rd.
49 B4 Restalrig Pk.
49 B4 Restalrig Rd.
49 B4 Restalrig Ter.
45 A3 Richmond La.
45 A3 Richmond Pl.
44 A1 Richmond Ter.
44 A1 Riego St.
48 B2 Rillbank Cres.
44 B2 Rillbank Ter.
48 C1 Rintoul Pl.
43 B4 Ritchie Pl.
43 B3 Riversdale Cres.
43 A3 Riversdale Gro.
43 A3 Riversdale Rd.
43 C3 Robbs Loan
43 C3 Robbs Loan Gro.
43 B3 Robertson Av.
45 A3 Robertsons Clo.
   Cowgate
45 A3 Robertsons Ct.
47 B4 Rocheid Pk.
48 B1 Rocheid Path
44 C1 Rochester Ter.
48 C2 Rodney St.
49 A3 Ronaldsons Wharf
   Bridge St.
44 A1 Rosebank Cotts.
44 A1 Rosebank Gdns.
44 A1 Rosebank Gro.
48 A1 Rosebank Rd.
43 A4 Rosebery Cres.
43 A4 Rosebery Crescent
   La.
   Rosebery Cres.
43 B3 Roseburn Av.
43 A4 Roseburn Cliff
43 A3 Roseburn Cres.
43 A3 Roseburn Dr.

43 A3 Roseburn Gdns.
43 A3 Roseburn Pl.
43 B3 Roseburn St.
43 A3 Roseburn Ter.
44 A1 Rosemount Bldgs.
44 B2 Roseneath Pl.
   Marchmont Cres.
44 B2 Roseneath St.
44 B2 Roseneath Ter.
45 B3 Rose Pk.
44 A1 Rose Street N. La.
44 A1 Rose Street S. La.
44 A1 Rose St.
49 B4 Rosevale Pl.
49 B4 Rosevale Ter.
48 A2 Roseville Gdns.
42 C3 Ross Gdns.
49 C4 Rossie Pl.
44 C2 Rosslyn Cres.
49 B3 Rosslyn Ter.
45 C3 Ross Pl.
43 A4 Rothesay Mews
44 A1 Rothesay Pl.
44 A1 Rothesay Ter.
42 B1 Roull Pl.
45 A3 Roxburgh Pl.
45 A3 Roxburgh St.
45 A3 Roxburgh Ter.
   Drummond St.
48 C1 Royal Circus
48 C2 Royal Cres.
49 C4 Royal Park Pl.
49 C4 Royal Park Ter.
49 C3 Royal Ter.
49 C3 Royal Terrace Mews
47 A3 Royston Mains Av.
47 A3 Royston Mains Cres.
47 A4 Royston Mains Gdns.
47 A4 Royston Mains Grn.
47 A3 Royston Mains Pl.
47 A4 Royston Mains Rd.
47 A3 Royston Mains St.
48 B1 Royston Ter.
48 A1 Russell Pl.
43 A4 Russell Rd.
44 A1 Rutland Ct.
44 A1 Rutland Ct. La.
44 A1 Rutland Pl.
   West End
44 A1 Rutland Sq.
44 A1 Rutland St.
49 B4 Ryehill Av.
49 B4 Ryehill Gdns.
49 B4 Ryehill Gro.
49 B4 Ryehill Pl.
49 B4 Ryehill Ter.

S
44 C2 St. Albans Rd.
49 B4 St. Andrews St.
48 C2 St. Andrew Sq.
49 A3 St. Anthony Ct.
   St. Anthony St.
49 A3 St. Anthony Pl.
   Henderson St.
49 A3 St. Anthony St.
48 C1 St. Bernards Cres.
48 C1 St. Bernards Pl.
   Saunders St.
48 C1 St. Bernards Row
42 B2 St. Catherines Gdns.
43 B3 St. Catherines Pl.
49 B4 St. Clair Av.
49 B4 St. Clair Pl.
49 B4 St. Clair Rd.
49 B4 St. Clair St.
44 A1 St. Colme St.
44 A1 St. Davids Pl.
   Morrison St.
44 A1 St. Davids Ter.
44 A2 St. Giles St.
48 C2 St. James Pl.
42 B1 St. Johns Av.
42 B1 St. Johns Cres.
42 B1 St. Johns Gdns.
43 A3 St. Johns Hill
45 A3 St. Johns Pl.
   Holyrood Rd.
42 B1 St. Johns Ter.
45 A3 St. John St.

45 B3 St. Leonards Crag
   St. Leonards La.
45 B3 St. Leonards Bank
45 B3 St. Leonards Hill
45 B3 St. Leonards St.
44 C1 St. Margarets Rd.
44 C2 St. Margarets Pl.
45 A3 St. Marys St.
45 B3 St. Patrick Sq.
45 B3 St. Patrick St.
44 B1 St. Peters Bldgs.
   Gilmore Pl.
44 B1 St. Peters Pl.
   Viewforth
48 C1 St. Stephen Pl.
48 C1 St. Stephen St.
43 C4 St. Teresa Pl.
44 C2 St. Thomnas Rd.
48 C1 St. Vincent St.
49 A4 Salamander Pl.
49 A4 Salamander St.
49 B4 Salamander St.
   Claremont Pk.
45 B3 Salisbury Pl.
45 B3 Salisbury Rd.
45 A3 Salisbury Sq.
45 A3 Salisbury St.
49 C4 Salmond Pl.
46 A2 Salvesen Cres.
46 A2 Salvesen Gdns.
46 A2 Salvesen Gro.
46 A2 Salvesen Ter.
49 A3 Sandport
49 A3 Sandport Pl.
43 B4 Sauchie Bank
43 C3 Saughton Av.
42 C3 Saughton Cres.
42 B2 Saughton Gdns.
42 B2 Saughton Gro.
43 B3 Saughtonhall Av.
42 B2 Saughtonhall Av. W.
43 B3 Saughtonhall Circus
42 B2 Saughtonhall Cres.
43 B3 Saughtonhall Dr.
43 B3 Saughtonhall Gdns.
43 B3 Saughtonhall Gro.
42 B2 Saughtonhall Pl.
43 B3 Saughtonhall Ter.
42 B2 Saughton Loan
42 C1 Saughton Mains Av.
42 C1 Saughton Mains Dr.
42 C1 Saughton Mains Gdns.
42 C2 Saughton Mains Gro.
42 C1 Saughton Mains
   Loan
42 C1 Saughton Mains Pk.
42 C1 Saughton Mains Pl.
42 C1 Saughton Mains St.
42 C1 Saughton Mains Ter.
42 B2 Saughton Pk.
42 C1 Saughton Rd.
42 B1 Saughton Rd. N.
48 C1 Saunders St.
45 C3 Savile Rd.
45 C3 Savile Ter.
48 C1 Saxe Coburg Pl.
48 C1 Saxe Coburg St.
45 B3 Sciennes
45 B3 Sciennes Hill Pl.
   Sciennes
45 B3 Sciennes House Pl.
45 B3 Sciennes Pl.
   Sciennes
44 B2 Sciennes Rd.
45 B3 Sciennes St. E.
   Causewayside
48 C2 Scotland St.
47 C3 Seaforth Dr.
49 A4 Seaport St.
44 A1 Semple St.
45 B3 Seton Pl.
43 C4 Shaftesbury Pk.
43 C4 Shandon Cres.
43 C4 Shandon Pl.
43 C4 Shandon Rd.
43 C4 Shandon St.
43 C4 Shandon Ter.

44 A1 Shandwick Pl.
45 C4 Sharpdale
   Dalkeith Rd.
49 B3 Shaws Pl.
49 C3 Shaws Sq.
   Gayfield Sq.
49 B3 Shaws St.
   Shaws Pl.
49 B3 Shaws Ter.
49 A3 Sheriff Brae
49 A3 Sheriff Pk.
49 A4 Shore
49 A4 Shore Pl.
49 C3 Shrub Pl.
49 C3 Shrub Place La.
   Shrub Pl.
45 B3 Sienna Gdns.
46 B1 Silverknowes Av.
46 B1 Silverknowes Bank
46 B1 Silverknowes Brae
46 B1 Silverknowes Ct.
46 B1 Silverknowes Cres.
46 B1 Silverknowes Dell
46 B1 Silverknowes Dr.
46 B1 Silverknowes
   Eastway
46 A1 Silverknowes Gdns.
46 B2 Silverknowes Grn.
46 A1 Silverknowes Gro.
46 B1 Silverknowes Hill
46 B1 Silverknowes Loan
46 B2 Silverknowes
   Midway
46 B2 Silverknowes Neuk
46 A1 Silverknowes
   Parkway
46 A1 Silverknowes Pl.
46 A1 Silverknowes Rd.
46 B1 Silverknowes Rd. E.
46 B1 Silverknowes Rd. S.
46 B2 Silverknowes
   Southway
46 B1 Silverknowes Ter.
46 B2 Silverknowes Vw.
43 A3 Simon Sq.
49 C4 Sleigh Dr.
49 B3 Sloan St.
43 B3 Smithfield St.
49 B3 Smiths Pl.
44 A2 Society
   Chambers St.
44 A2 Solicitors Bldgs.
   Cowgate
49 B4 Somerset Pl.
42 B2 South Beechwood
44 A2 South Bridge
44 A1 South Charlotte St.
45 B3 South Clerk St.
48 C1 South College St.
48 C1 South East Circus Pl.
48 C2 South East
   Cumberland Street
   La.
48 C2 South East Thistle
   Street La.
49 A3 South Fort St.
43 C4 South Gillsland Rd.
44 C2 South Grays Clo.
45 C3 South Gray St.
47 C3 South Groathill Av.
44 A1 South La.
45 C3 South Lauder Rd.
48 C2 South Laverockbank
   Av.
47 C4 South Learmonth Av.
47 C4 South Learmonth
   Gdns.
49 B3 South Lorne Pl.
44 B2 South Meadow Wk.
44 C2 South Oswald Rd.
45 B3 South Oxford St.
48 C2 South St. Andrew St.
48 C2 South St. David St.
49 B3 South Sloan St.
48 A1 South Trinity Rd.
48 C2 South West
   Cumberland Street
   La.
48 C2 South West Thistle
   Street La.

48 A1 Spencer Pl.
45 B3 Spence St.
49 B3 Spey Street Mews
49 B3 Spey St.
49 A3 Spiers Pl.
45 B3 Spittalfield Cres.
  St. Leonards St.
44 A1 Spittal St.
44 B2 Spottiswoode Rd.
44 B2 Spottiswoode St.
49 B3 Springfield Bldgs.
  Springfield St.
49 B3 Springfield St.
49 C4 Spring Gdns.
44 C1 Springvalley Gdns.
44 C1 Springvalley Ter.
43 B4 Springwell Pl.
43 C4 Spylaw Rd.
44 C1 Stable La.
44 A1 Stafford St.
43 A3 Stair Pk.
43 A4 Stanhope Pl.
43 A4 Stanhope Pl.
  Stanhope Pl.
49 C4 Stanley Pl.
48 A2 Stanley Rd.
49 B3 Stanwell St.
48 A2 Starbank Rd.
42 B1 Station Rd.
49 B3 Steads Pl.
44 C1 Steels Pl.
42 C2 Stenhouse Av.
42 C2 Stenhouse Av. W.
42 C2 Stenhouse Cotts.
42 C2 Stenhouse Cres.
42 C2 Stenhouse Cross
42 C1 Stenhouse Dr.
42 C2 Stenhouse Gdns.
42 C2 Stenhouse Gdns. N.
42 C2 Stenhouse Gro.
42 C2 Stenhouse Mill
  Cres.
42 C2 Stenhouse Mill
42 C2 Stenhouse Muir Dr.
42 C2 Stenhouse Pl. E.
42 C2 Stenhouse Pl. W.
42 C2 Stenhouse Rd.
42 C2 Stenhouse St. E.
42 C1 Stenhouse St. W.
42 C2 Stenhouse Ter.
44 A2 Stevenlaws Clo.
  High St.
43 B3 Stevenson Av.
42 C2 Stevenson Dr.
43 B3 Stevenson Gro.
43 B3 Stevenson Rd.
43 B3 Stevenson Ter.
48 B2 Stewartfield
43 B3 Stewart Ter.
48 A1 Stirling Rd.
42 B1 Stoneyhill Farm Rd.
49 A3 Storries Alley
  Giles St.
46 C2 Strachan Gdns.
46 C2 Strachan Rd.
44 C1 Strathearn Pl.
42 C2 Strathearn Rd.
44 C2 Strathfillan Rd.
43 A3 Succoth Av.
43 A3 Succoth Ct.
43 A3 Succoth Gdns.
43 A3 Succoth Pk.
43 A3 Succoth Pl.
45 C3 Suffolk Rd.
48 C2 Summer Bank
49 B4 Summerfield Gdns.
49 B4 Summerfield Pl.
45 B3 Summerhall
45 B3 Summerhall Sq.
48 B2 Summer Pl.
48 A2 Summerside Pl.
48 A2 Summerside St.
43 A4 Sunbury Mews
43 A4 Sunbury Pl.
43 A4 Sunbury St.
49 C4 Sunnybank Pl.
49 C4 Sunnybank Ter.
  Sunnybank Pl.

49 C4 Sunnyside
45 A3 Surgeon Sq.
  Infirmary St.
43 A4 Surrey Pl.
  Borthwick Pl.
43 A4 Surrey Sq.
  Sutherland St.
43 A4 Sutherland St.
49 A3 Swanfield
42 B1 Sycamore Gdns.
42 B1 Sycamore Ter.
44 B2 Sylvan Pl.

T
48 B2 Tanfield
48 B2 Tanfield La.
44 B2 Tantallon Pl.
44 B1 Tarvit St.
49 A3 Taylor Gdns.
  Great Junction St.
49 C4 Taylor Pl.
43 B4 Tay St.
43 B4 Telfer Subway
47 B3 Telford Dr.
47 B3 Telford Gdns.
47 B3 Telford Pl.
46 C2 Telford Rd.
43 B4 Temple Park Cres.
49 B3 Tennant St.
48 C1 Teviotdale Pl.
44 A2 Teviot Pl.
44 A2 Teviot Row
49 A3 Bowling Green,
  The,
44 A3 Quilts, The,
44 B2 Thirlestane La.
44 B2 Thirlestane Rd.
48 C2 Thistle Ct.
  Thistle St.
48 B1 Thistle Pl.
48 C2 Thistle St.
49 A3 Thomas Fraser Ct.
  Cromwell Pl.
44 A2 Thomsons Ct.
  Grassmarket
44 B1 Thorneybauk
49 B4 Thorntree Side
49 B4 Thorntree St.
49 B4 Thornville Ter.
44 A4 Timber Bush
49 B3 Tinto Pl.
44 C1 Tipperlinn Rd.
44 A1 Tobago Pl.
  Morrison St.
49 A4 Tolbooth Wynd
44 B1 Tollcross
44 A1 Torphichen Pl.
44 A1 Torphichen St.
49 A4 Tower Pl.
49 A4 Tower Street La.
49 A4 Tower St.
49 A3 Trafalgar La.
49 A3 Trafalgar St.
42 B1 Traquair Pk. E.
42 B1 Traquair Pk. W.
48 A1 Trinity Cres.
48 A1 Trinity Gro.
48 A1 Trinity Rd.
44 A2 Tron Sq.
44 A2 Turnbulls Entry
  Potterrow
42 B1 Tylers Acre Av.
42 B1 Tylers Acre Gdns.
42 B1 Tylers Acre Rd.
43 B4 Tynecastle La.
43 B4 Tynecastle Pl.
43 B4 Tynecastle Ter.
  Gorgie Rd.

U
45 A3 Union Ct.
  Richmond Pl.
49 C3 Union Pl.
49 C3 Union St.

44 A2 Upper Bow
43 A4 Upper Coltbridge
  Ter.
48 C1 Upper Dean Ter.
44 B1 Upper Gilmore Pl.
44 B1 Upper Gilmore Ter.
45 B3 Upper Gray St.
49 C3 Upper Greenside
  La.
  Greenside Row
44 B1 Upper Grove Pl.
45 A3 Upper Viewcraig
  Row
  Waterston Av.

V
44 B1 Valleyfield St.
49 B4 Vanburgh Pl.
48 C1 Veitchs Sq.
  St. Bernards Row
44 A2 Vennel
45 C3 Ventnor Ter.
44 A2 Victoria St.
44 A2 Victoria Ter.
  Victoria St.
45 A3 Viewcraig Gdns.
45 A3 Viewcraig St.
44 B1 Viewforth
44 B1 Viewforth Gdns.
44 B1 Viewforth Sq.
44 B1 Viewforth Ter.
49 C4 Violet Bank
  Spring Gdns.
43 B4 Violet Ter.
  Slateford Rd.
46 B2 Vivian Ter.

W
49 B3 Waddell Pl.
44 A1 Walker St.
44 A1 Walker Ter.
  Dalry Pl.
48 A1 Wardie Av.
47 A4 Wardieburn Dr.
47 A4 Wardieburn Pl. E.
47 A4 Wardieburn Pl. N.
47 A4 Wardieburn Pl. S.
47 A4 Wardieburn Pl. W.
47 A4 Wardieburn Rd.
47 A4 Wardieburn St. E.
47 A4 Wardieburn St. W.
47 A4 Wardieburn Ter.
48 A1 Wardie Cres.
48 A1 Wardie Dell
48 A1 Wardie Gro.
48 A1 Wardie Pk.
48 A1 Wardie Rd.
48 A1 Wardie Sq.
48 A1 Wardie Steps
  Wardie Sq.
43 B4 Wardlaw Pl.
43 B4 Wardlaw St.
43 B4 Wardlaw Ter.
44 B1 Warrender Park
  Cres.
44 B2 Warrender Park
  Rd.
44 B2 Warrender Park
  Ter.
48 B2 Warriston Av.
48 B2 Warriston Cres.
48 B1 Warriston Dr.
48 B1 Warriston Gdns.
48 B1 Warriston Gro.
48 B2 Warriston Rd.
48 B2 Warriston Rd.
48 B1 Warriston Ter.
43 B4 Washington La.
43 B4 Washington St.
48 C2 Waterloo Pl.
43 A3 Waterside
  Coltbridge Av.
44 A4 Water St.
45 C3 Watertoun Rd.
43 B4 Watson Cres.
  Yeaman Pl.

44 A2 Waverley Bridge
44 A2 Waverley Market
  Princes St.
49 C4 Waverley Pk.
49 C4 Waverley Park Ter.
44 A2 Waverley Pl.
44 A2 Waverley Steps
  Princes St.
49 B4 Wellington Pl.
49 C3 Wellington St.
48 C1 Wemyss Pl.
48 C1 Wemyss Place
  Mews
  Wemyss Pl.
45 A3 West Adam St.
48 B2 West Annandale
  St.
43 B4 West Approach
  Rd.
45 A3 West Arthur St.
44 A2 West Bow
49 A3 West Bowling
  Green St.
43 B4 West Bryson Rd.
44 B1 West Castle Rd.
43 A4 West Catherine Pl.
44 A4 West Coates
44 A2 West College St.
47 C3 West Ct.
49 A3 West Cromwell St.
  Commercial St.
49 A3 West Cromwell St.
  Admiralty St.
45 B3 West
  Crosscauseway
44 A1 West End
43 B4 West End Pl.
43 A4 Wester Coates Av.
43 A4 Wester Coates
  Gdns.
43 A4 Wester Coates Pl.
43 A4 Wester Coates Rd.
43 A4 Wester Coates Ter.
46 B2 Wester Drylaw Av.
46 B2 Wester Drylaw Dr.
47 B3 Wester Drylaw Dri.
46 B2 Wester Drylaw Pl.
47 C3 Wester Drylaw
  Row
42 A2 Western Corner
  Saughtonhall Dr.
43 A3 Western Gdns.
43 A3 Western Pl.
43 A3 Western Ter.
47 B4 West Ferryfield
43 B3 Westfield Av.
43 B3 Westfield Ct.
43 B3 Westfield Rd.
43 B3 Westfield St.
43 B4 West Fountain Pl.
44 C2 West Grange
  Gdns.
46 A2 West Granton
  Cres.
47 A3 West Granton Dr.
47 A3 West Granton
  Gdns.
46 A2 West Granton Grn.
47 A3 West Granton Gro.
47 A3 West Granton Loan
46 A2 West Granton Pl.
47 A3 West Granton Rd.
47 A3 West Granton Row
47 A3 West Granton Ter.
47 A3 West Granton Vw.
44 B1 Westhall Gdns.
44 A1 West Maitland St.
45 C3 West Mayfield
44 B2 West Meadow Wk.
49 C3 West Montgomery
  Pl.
45 B3 West Newington
  Pl.
45 A3 West Nicolson St.
49 C3 West Norton Pl.
  London Rd.
43 B4 West Park Pl.

47 B3 West Pilton Av.
46 A2 West Pilton Bank
47 A3 West Pilton Circus
46 A2 West Pilton Cotts.
  Pennywell Rd.
46 A2 West Pilton Cres.
47 A3 West Pilton
  Crossway
47 A3 West Pilton Dri.
47 A3 West Pilton Gdns.
47 A3 West Pilton Gro.
47 A3 West Pilton Lea
47 A3 West Pilton Loan
47 A3 West Pilton Pk.
47 A3 West Pilton Pl.
47 A3 West Pilton Ri.
47 A3 West Pilton St.
47 A3 West Pilton Ter.
47 B3 West Pilton Vw.
44 A2 West Port
45 B3 West Preston St.
48 C2 West Register St.
44 C2 West Relugas Rd.
45 A3 West Richmond St.
45 C3 West Savile Rd.
45 C3 West Savile Ter.
47 B4 West Webeside
47 B4 West Winnelstrae
47 B4 West Woods
43 B3 Wheatfield Pl.
43 B3 Wheatfield Rd.
43 B4 Wheatfield Ter.
45 A3 White Horse Clo.
44 B1 Whitehouse Loan
42 B1 Whitehouse Ter.
43 B4 White Park
42 B2 Whitson Cres.
42 B2 Whitson Gro.
42 B2 Whitson Pl. E.
42 B2 Whitson Pl. W.
42 B2 Whitson Rd.
42 B2 Whitson Ter.
42 B2 Whitson Wk.
42 B2 Whitson Way
49 C4 Whyte Pl.
44 A1 William Street La.
  N.E.
  William St.
44 A1 William Street La.
  N.W.
  William St.
44 A1 William Street La.
  S.E.
  William St.
44 A1 William Street La.
  S.W.
  William St.
44 A1 William St.
48 A2 Willow Bank Row
45 B3 Windmill Pl.
49 C3 Windsor St.
49 C4 Wishaw Ter.
49 B4 Woodbine Ter.
44 C1 Woodburn Pl.
  Canaan La.
44 C1 Woodburn Ter.
49 B4 Woodville Ter.
44 B1 Wrights Houses
44 C2 Wyvern Pk.

Y
49 A3 Yardheads
43 B4 Yeaman La.
43 B4 Yeaman Pl.
48 C2 York Bldgs.
  Queen St.
48 C1 York La.
48 C2 York Pl.
48 A2 York Rd.
44 A1 Young Street La. N.
44 A1 Young Street La. S.
44 A1 Young St.

Z
48 A1 Zetland Pl.

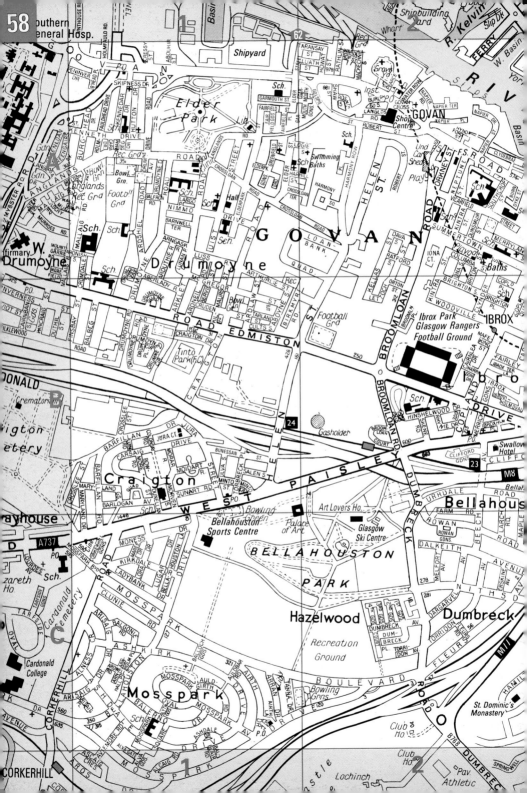

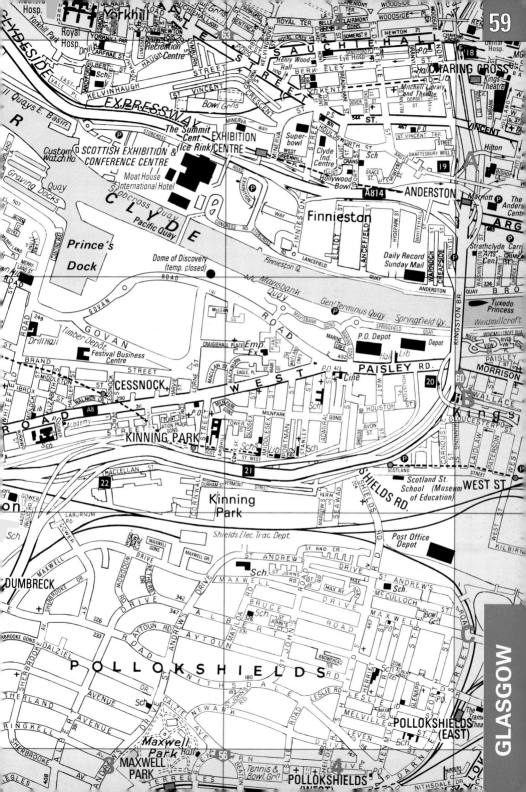

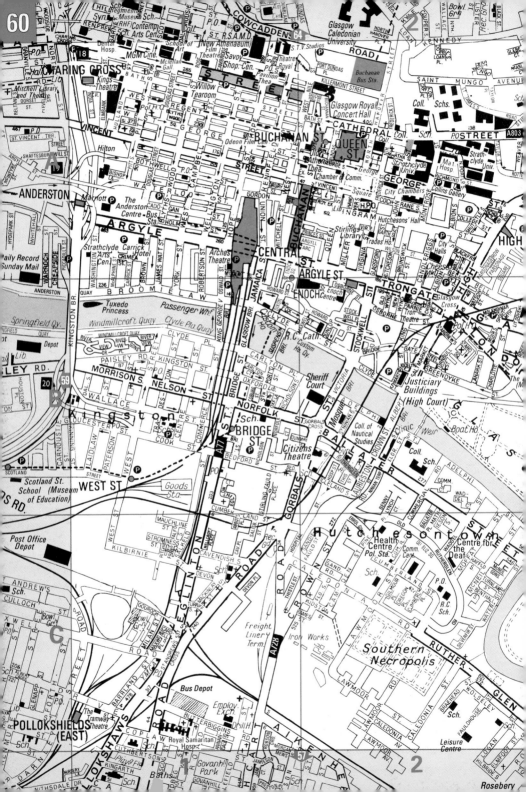

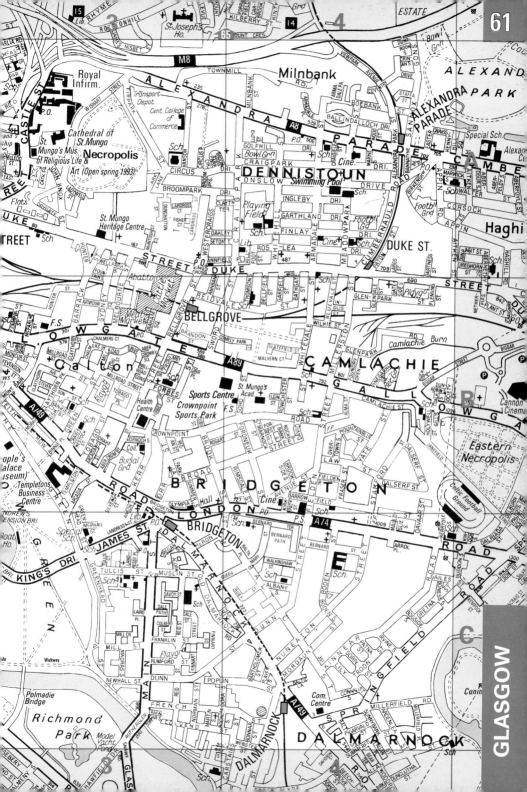

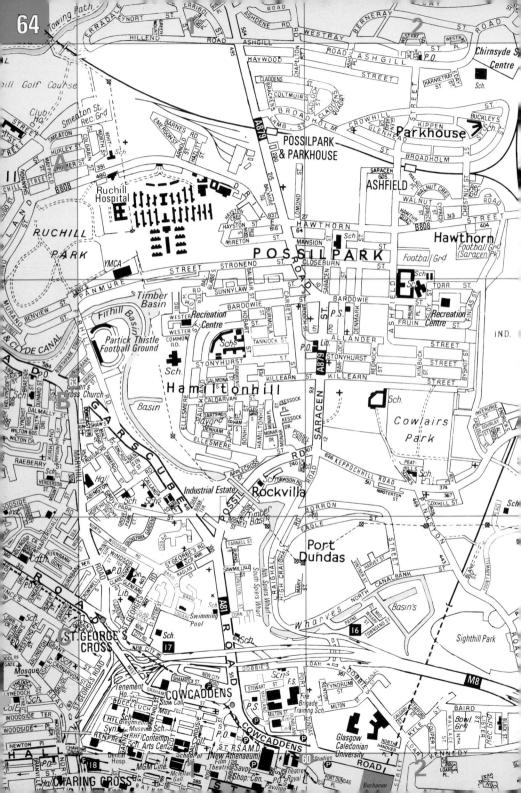

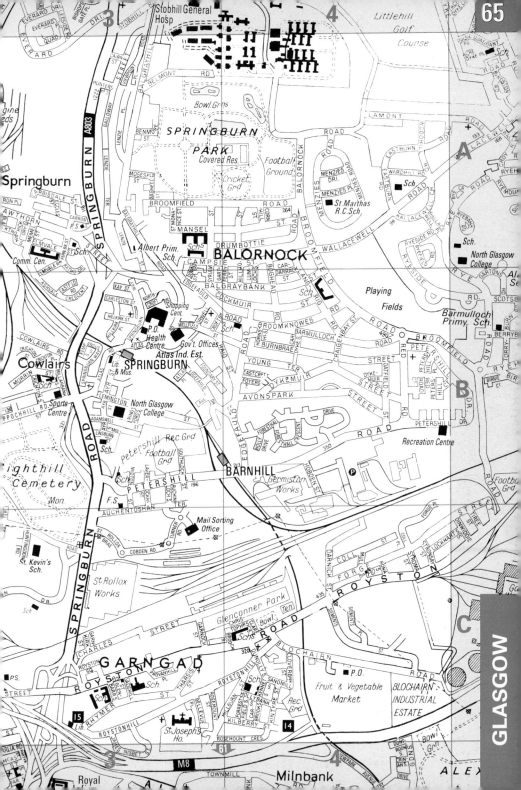

INDEX TO STREET NAMES

62 B1 Abbey Dr.
56 A2 Abbot St.
Frankfort St.
60 C1 Abbotsford La.
Cumberland St.
60 C1 Abbotsford Pl.
61 B3 Abercromby Dr.
61 B3 Abercromby Sq.
61 B3 Abercromby St.
58 A1 Aberlady Rd.
64 B1 Abington St.
58 A1 Aboukir St.
58 B1 Aboyne St.
61 C3 Acorn Ct.
Acorn St.
61 C3 Acorn St.
60 A1 Adams Ct. La.
Howard St.
65 B3 Adamswell St.
63 B3 Addison Rd.
60 B2 Adelphi St.
59 B4 Admiral St.
57 B3 Advie Pl.
Prospecthill Rd.
56 B2 Afton St.
62 A1 Aigas Cotts.
Crow Rd.
60 C1 Aikenhead Rd.
56 B2 Ailsa Dr.
60 B2 Aird's La.
Bridgegate
62 B2 Airlie St.
56 C2 Airlour Rd.
58 C1 Airth Dr.
58 C1 Airth La.
58 C1 Airth Pl.
62 B1 Airthrey Av.
62 A1 Albany Cotts.
Crow Rd.
61 C4 Albany St.
56 A2 Albert Av.
60 B2 Albert Bri.
59 C4 Albert Ct.
Albert Dr.
59 C4 Albert Cross
56 A1 Albert Dr.
57 A3 Albert Rd.
63 B3 Alberta Ter.
Saltoun St.
60 A2 Albion St.
56 C1 Alder Pl.
56 C1 Alder Rd.
61 A4 Alexandra Ct.
Roebank St.
61 A4 Alexandra Cross
Duke St.
61 A4 Alexandra Par.
61 A4 Alexandra Pk. St.
64 B2 Alford St.
63 B3 Alfred Ter.
Cecil St.
56 B2 Algie St.
61 C4 Allan Pl.
64 B2 Allander St.
57 A3 Allison Pl.
Prince Edward St.
57 A3 Allison St.
56 C1 Alloway Rd.
61 B4 Alma St.
58 C1 Alness Cres.
61 B3 Alston La.
Claythorn St.
63 B3 Alton Gdns.
Great George St.
58 C1 Alyth Gdns.
63 A4 Amisfield St.
62 A1 Ancaster Dr.
64 B1 Ancroft St.
62 C2 Anderson St.
60 A1 Anderston Cross
Cen.
Anderston Quay
59 B4 Angus St.
65 B3 Annan St.
60 C1 Annandale St.
58 A1 Annbank St.
57 A3 Annette St.
61 A4 Annfield Pl.
62 A1 Anniesland Mans.
Ancaster Dr.
61 C3 Anson St.
60 A1 Anthony St.
Cadogan St.
61 A4 Appin Rd.
64 B1 Appleby St.
64 B1 Applecross St.

62 C2 Apsley La.
62 C2 Apsley St.
63 A3 Aray St.
61 B3 Arcadia St.
57 A3 Ardbeg St.
61 C4 Ardenlea St.
62 C2 Ardery St.
Apsley St.
63 A3 Ardessie Pl.
58 B1 Ardlaw St.
56 C2 Ardle Rd.
57 B4 Ardmay Cres.
57 B4 Ardmory Av.
57 B4 Ardnahoe Av.
57 B4 Ardnahoe Pl.
58 A1 Ardneil Rd.
58 A1 Ardnish St.
58 B2 Ardo Gdns.
58 A1 Ardoch St.
58 A1 Ardshiel Rd.
58 C1 Arduthie Rd.
58 A1 Ardwell Rd.
60 A1 Argyle St.
60 A1 Argyll Arc.
58 C1 Arisaig Dr.
58 C1 Arisaig Pl.
61 A3 Ark La.
58 B1 Arklet Rd.
61 A4 Arlington St.
Townmill Rd.
60 C2 Armadale Ct.
60 C2 Armadale Path
61 A4 Armadale Pl.
61 A4 Armadale St.
61 B3 Armour St.
58 A1 Arngask Rd.
58 C1 Arnhall Pl.
58 C1 Arnholm Pl.
64 A1 Arnold St.
62 A2 Arnwood Dr.
63 B3 Arriochmill Rd.
Kelvin Dr.
61 A4 Arrol Pl.
63 C3 Arthur St.
58 A1 Arthurlie St.
57 B3 Arundel Dr.
57 A3 Ascog St.
57 A3 Ascot Av.
62 A2 Ascot Ct.
62 A2 Ashburton Rd.
58 C1 Ashdale Dr.
64 B2 Ashfield St.
64 A2 Ashgill Pl.
64 A2 Ashgill Rd.
58 C1 Ashkirk Dr.
63 C4 Ashley La.
Woodlands Rd.
63 C4 Ashley St.
63 C3 Ashmore Rd.
63 C3 Ashton Gdns.
University Av.
63 C3 Ashton La.
University Av.
63 B3 Ashton Rd.
Byres Rd.
63 C3 Ashton Rd.
University Av.
63 C3 Ashton Ter.
University Av.
56 B1 Ashtree Rd.
65 B4 Ashvale Cres.
Foresthall Dr.
65 B4 Aspen Dr.
Foresthall Dr.
63 B3 Athole Gdns.
63 B3 Athole La.
Saltoun St.
65 B3 Atlas Pl.
65 B3 Atlas Rd.
62 C1 Auchentorlie St.
Dumbarton Rd.
65 C3 Auchentoshan
Ter.
65 B3 Auchinloch St.
64 B1 Auckland St.
58 C1 Auldbar Rd.
58 C1 Auldgirth Rd.
56 C1 Auldhouse Av.
56 C1 Auldhouse Ter.
Auldhouse Rd.
62 A1 Austen La.
Skaterig La.
62 A1 Austen Rd.
61 B4 Avenue St.
61 B4 Avenuepark St.
59 B4 Avon St.
65 B4 Avonspark St.

56 C2 Aylmer Rd.
65 B3 Ayr St.
59 C3 Aytoun Rd.

B

56 A3 Bagnell St.
61 B3 Bain Sq.
Bain St.
61 B3 Bain St.
64 C2 Baird St.
64 B1 Bairdsbrae
Possil Rd.
56 A2 Baker Pl.
Baker St.
56 A2 Baker St.
60 B1 Balaclava St.
McAlpine St.
58 B1 Balbeg St.
59 B4 Balcarres Av.
63 B3 Balerno Dr.
63 A3 Balfour St.
63 A3 Balfron Rd.
64 B1 Balgair St.
64 B1 Balglass St.
56 B1 Balgonie Rd.
65 B4 Balgraybank St.
65 A3 Balgrayhill Rd.
63 C4 Baliol La.
Woodlands Rd.
63 C4 Baliol St.
60 C2 Ballater Pl.
60 C2 Ballater St.
61 A4 Ballindalloch Dr.
57 B3 Balloch Gdns.
57 B3 Ballogie Rd.
57 A3 Balmoral Cres.
Queens Dr.
65 A4 Balmore Sq.
62 B1 Balshagray Av.
62 B1 Balshagray Cres.
62 B1 Balshagray Dr.
62 B1 Balshagray La.
62 B1 Balshagray Pl.
Balshagray Av.
61 C4 Baltic Ct.
61 C4 Baltic La.
61 C3 Baltic Pl.
61 C4 Baltic St.
56 A2 Balvicar Dr.
56 A2 Balvicar St.
62 B2 Banavie Rd.
63 C4 Bank St.
57 B3 Bankhall St.
57 B3 Bankier St.
61 A4 Bannatyne Av.
57 C3 Barbreck Rd.
Pollokshaws Rd.
65 A3 Barclay St.
Balgrayhill Rd.
64 B1 Bardowie St.
58 B1 Barfillan Dr.
58 B1 Barfillan Rd.
64 B2 Barloch St.
58 B1 Barlogan Av.
58 B1 Barlogan Quad.
65 C4 Barmulloch Rd.
61 C4 Barnard Ter.
57 B3 Barnes Rd.
65 B4 Barnhill Dr.
Foresthall Dr.
58 A1 Barnwell Ter.
62 A2 Baronald Dr.
62 A2 Baronald Gate
64 B1 Barr St.
61 B3 Barrack St.
61 B3 Barrington Dr.
60 C1 Barrland St.
61 C4 Barrowfield St.
61 C4 Bartholomew St.
60 A1 Bath La.
Blythswood St.
59 A4 Bath La. W.
North St.
60 A1 Bath St.
58 A3 Bathgate St.
60 C1 Batson St.
61 B4 Battle Pl.
65 C4 Battlefield Av.
65 C4 Battlefield Cres.
65 C4 Battlefield Gdns.
65 C4 Battlefield Rd.
62 C1 Beaconsfield Rd.
62 C1 Bearsden Rd.
56 A2 Beaton Rd.

56 C1 Beaufort Av.
61 A3 Beauly Pl.
63 C3 Beaumont Gate
60 B1 Bedford La.
60 B1 Bedford Row
Dunmore St.
60 B1 Bedford St.
65 B3 Bedlay St.
Petershill Rd.
58 C2 Beech Av.
62 B1 Beechwood Av.
Beechwood Dr.
62 B1 Beechwood Dr.
62 B1 Beechwood Pl.
Beechwood Dr.
62 C2 Beith St.
63 B4 Belgrave La.
63 B4 Belgrave Ter.
Belgrave Ter.
63 B3 Belhaven Cres. La.
Lorraine Rd.
63 B3 Belhaven Ter.
63 B3 Belhaven Ter. W.
60 A2 Bell St.
58 C1 Bellahouston Dr.
58 C1 Bellahouston La.
58 C1 Belleisle St.
65 C3 Bellevue Pl.
61 B4 Bellfield St.
61 B3 Bellgrove St.
63 B3 Bellshaugh Gdns.
63 B3 Bellshaugh La.
63 B3 Bellshaugh Pl.
63 B3 Bellshaugh Rd.
56 B2 Bellwood St.
61 B4 Belmont Cres.
63 B4 Belmont La.
Great Western Rd.
61 B4 Belmont St.
65 A3 Belmont St.
61 B4 Beltane St.
63 C3 Benalder St.
61 B3 Bengal Pl.
Christian St.
56 B1 Bengal St.
58 A3 Benmore St.
57 A4 Bennan Sq.
60 B2 Benthall St.
60 C2 Bentinck St.
63 C4 Benview St.
62 B1 Beresford Av.
59 A4 Berkeley St.
63 C4 Berkeley Ter. La.
Elderslie St.
61 C4 Bernard Path
61 C4 Bernard St.
61 C4 Bernard Ter.
57 C3 Berridale Av.
56 A2 Bertram St.
58 B1 Bervie St.
58 C1 Beverley Rd.
61 B4 Biggar Pl.
61 B4 Biggar St.
62 B1 Binnie Pl.
61 B3 Birkenshaw St.
61 B3 Birkmyre Rd.
58 B1 Birness Dr.
58 B1 Birness St.
61 B3 Bishop St.
65 A3 Bishopsgate Dr.
65 A3 Bishopsgate Gdns.
65 A3 Bishopsgate Pl.
65 A3 Bishopsgate Rd.
64 C2 Black St.
59 B4 Blackburn St.
60 A2 Blackfriars St.
63 C3 Blackie St.
65 B3 Blackthorn St.
62 B3 Blairatholl Av.
57 B3 Blairatholl Gdns.
60 A2 Blairbeth Dr.
57 B3 Blairhall Av.
64 C1 Blane St.
61 B3 Blantyre St.
64 C1 Blochairn Rd.
60 A1 Bluevale St.
60 A1 Blythswood Ct.
Cadogan St.
60 A1 Blythswood Sq.
60 B1 Blythswood St.
61 A3 Boden St.
65 B4 Boghead Rd.

61 C4 Bogside St.
61 A3 Boleyn Rd.
57 B4 Bolivar Ter.
57 B3 Bolton Dr.
61 C4 Bonawe St.
61 C4 Boness St.
58 A1 Bonhill St.
64 B1 Bonnar St.
62 A1 Borden La.
62 A1 Borden Rd.
64 A2 Borron St.
56 B2 Boswell Ct.
63 B3 Botanic Cres.
60 A1 Bothwell La.
West Campbell St.
60 A1 Bothwell St.
63 C4 Bothwell Ter.
Bank St.
65 B4 Bower St.
65 B4 Bowling Grn. Rd.
57 A3 Bowman St.
61 A3 Bowmont Gdns.
63 B3 Bowmont Ter.
58 B1 Bowmore Rd.
57 A3 Boyd St.
64 A1 Bracken St.
63 A3 Bracora Pl.
Glenfinnan Dr.
63 A3 Bradfield Av.
60 C2 Braehead St.
63 C3 Braemar St.
63 B4 Braeside St.
64 C1 Braid Sq.
56 C1 Braid St.
59 B3 Brand St.
63 A3 Brandon St.
63 A4 Brassey St.
59 A4 Breadalbane St.
64 B2 Brechin St.
56 C1 Brereton St.
56 C1 Briar Rd.
60 B1 Bridge St.
60 B1 Bridgegate
61 B3 Bridgeton Cross
62 C2 Brighton Pl.
65 A3 Brighton St.
57 B3 Brisbane St.
58 B2 Briton St.
61 B3 Broad Pl.
61 B3 Broad St.
64 C2 Broadford St.
Harvey St.
64 A1 Broadholm St.
57 C3 Broadwood Dr.
65 C4 Brodick St.
61 B3 Brook St.
56 C1 Brooklea Dr.
56 C1 Brookside St.
56 C1 Broom Rd.
65 B4 Broomfield Av.
Broomfield Rd.
65 A3 Broomfield Pl.
Broomfield Rd.
65 A3 Broomfield Rd.
62 C1 Broomhill Av.
63 A3 Broomhill Cres.
62 B1 Broomhill Dr.
62 B1 Broomhill Gdns.
62 B1 Broomhill La.
62 C1 Broomhill Path
62 C1 Broomhill Pl.
62 C1 Broomhill Ter.
60 B1 Broomielaw
65 B4 Broomknowes Rd.
65 B2 Broomloan Ct.
58 B2 Broomloan Pl.
58 B2 Broomloan Rd.
64 B1 Brown St.
64 B1 Brownlie St.
59 C4 Bruce Rd.
60 A2 Brunswick St.
57 B3 Brunton St.
64 C1 Buccleuch La.
Scott St.
60 B1 Buccleuch St.
60 B1 Buchan St.
Norfolk St.
60 A1 Buchanan St.
63 B3 Buckingham
Bldgs.
Great Western Rd.
63 B3 Buckingham St.

63 B3 Buckingham Ter.
64 A2 Buckley St.
58 B1 Bunessan St.
63 C3 Bunhouse Rd.
62 C2 Burgh Hall La.
Fortrose St.
62 C2 Burgh Hall St.
63 B3 Burgh La.
Vinicombe St.
62 A1 Burghead Dr.
58 A1 Burghead Pl.
58 A1 Burleigh St.
62 A1 Burlington Av.
62 A2 Burmola St.
63 C4 Burnbank Gdns.
61 A3 Burnbank Pl.
Drygate
63 C4 Burnbank Ter.
65 B4 Burnbrae St.
59 A3 Burndyke Ct.
59 A3 Burndyke Sq.
58 A2 Burndyke St.
56 C2 Burnhead Rd.
60 A3 Burnhouse St.
64 C1 Burns St.
61 A3 Burrells La.
High St.
56 C2 Burrelton Rd.
57 A3 Burton La.
Langside Rd.
63 C3 Bute Gdns.
60 C1 Butterbiggins Rd.
56 A2 Butterfield Pl.
Pollokshaws Rd.
63 C3 Byres Rd.
62 C1 Byron La.
Sandeman St.
62 C1 Byron St.
64 B2 Byshot St.

C

60 A1 Cadogan St.
60 A1 Cadzow St.
Cadogan St.
62 C2 Caird Dr.
65 A3 Cairn St.
56 C1 Cairngorm Rd.
58 B2 Cairnlea Dr.
63 B4 Caithness St.
64 B1 Caldarvan St.
64 B3 Calder St.
56 C1 Calderwood Rd.
63 C3 Caledon La.
Highburgh Rd.
63 C3 Caledon St.
60 C2 Caledonia Av.
60 C2 Caledonia Rd.
63 C4 Caledonia Cres.
63 B3 Caledonian
Mans.
Great Western Rd.
64 C2 Calgary St.
61 B3 Callander St.
61 B3 Calton Entry
Gallowgate
63 A3 Cambridge Dr.
Glenfinnan Dr.
63 A3 Cambridge La.
Cambridge St.
64 C1 Cambridge St.
60 A1 Cambridge St.
64 C2 Camden St.
64 B1 Cameron St.
64 B1 Camlachie St.
64 B1 Camperdown St.
Garscube Rd.
65 B2 Camphill Av.
65 A3 Campsie St.
64 C2 Canal St.
60 C2 Candleriggs
59 A3 Canting Way
58 A1 Cara Dr.
64 B1 Carberry Rd.
64 B1 Carbeth St.
65 C4 Carbisdale St.
65 C4 Carbrook St.
61 A3 Cardarrach St.
59 A4 Carding La.
Argyle St.
61 A3 Cardross Ct.
61 A3 Cardross St.
60 C1 Cardwell St.
65 B4 Cardyke St.
63 A3 Carfin St.
59 A3 Carfrae St.
59 B3 Carillon Rd.
56 C1 Carlaverock Rd.

65 B3 Carleston St.
Atlas Rd.
64 B2 Carlisle St.
60 B1 Carlton Ct.
60 B1 Carlton Pl.
63 B4 Carlton Ter.
Wilton St.
56 B1 Carment Dr.
56 B1 Carment La.
56 B2 Carmichael Pl.
58 B2 Carmichael St.
57 C3 Carmunnock La.
Madison Av.
57 B3 Carmunnock Rd.
57 C4 Carna Dr.
63 C4 Carnarvon St.
64 C1 Carnbroe St.
59 B4 Carnoustie St.
56 C2 Carnwath Av.
63 A3 Carrbridge Dr.
Glenfinnan Dr.
60 A1 Carrick St.
63 C4 Carrington St.
64 A2 Carron Cres.
65 A3 Carron Pl.
65 A3 Carron St.
58 B1 Carsaig Dr.
56 A2 Carswell Gdns.
56 B2 Cartha St.
57 B3 Cartside Quad.
56 B2 Cartside St.
56 B2 Cartvale Rd.
60 A2 Castle Cres. N. Ct.
Royal Ex. Sq.
61 A3 Castle St.
62 A1 Castlebank Ct.
62 C2 Castlebank Cres.
Meadowside St.
62 A1 Castlebank Gdns.
62 C1 Castlebank St.
62 A1 Castlebank Vills.
57 B3 Cathcart Rd.
60 A2 Cathedral Ct.
Rottenrow E.
60 A2 Cathedral La.
Cathedral St.
61 A3 Cathedral Sq.
60 A2 Cathedral St.
59 A4 Catherine Pl.
Hydepark St.
56 B2 Cathkin Rd.
57 B3 Cathkinview Rd.
60 C1 Cavendish Pl.
60 C1 Cavendish St.
59 B4 Cecil Pl.
Paisley Rd. W.
63 B3 Cecil St.
64 C1 Cedar Ct.
64 C1 Cedar St.
62 C1 Central Av.
Broomhill Ter.
60 A1 Central Chambers
Hope St.
60 A1 Central Sta.
60 B1 Centre St.
59 B3 Cessnock St.
58 A1 Chachan Dr.
Skipness Dr.
61 B3 Chalmers Ct.
61 B3 Chalmers Gate
Claythorn St.
61 B3 Chalmers Pl.
Claythorn St.
61 B3 Chalmers St.
62 A1 Chamberlain La.
62 A1 Chamberlain Rd.
62 C2 Chancellor St.
63 A4 Chapel St.
64 A1 Chapelton St.
57 A3 Chapman St.
Allison St.
63 C4 Charing Cross
59 A4 Charing Cross La.
Granville St.
65 C3 Charles St.
60 B2 Charlotte La.
London Rd.
60 B2 Charlotte La. S.
Charlotte St.
60 B2 Charlotte St.
59 A4 Cheapside St.
62 A2 Chelmsford Dr.
56 C2 Cherrybank Rd.
62 A2 Chesterfield Av.
64 A2 Chestnut St.
56 C1 Cheviot Rd.
60 B2 Chisholm St.
56 B1 Christian St.
65 C4 Christopher St.
57 A3 Church La.
Victoria Rd.
63 C3 Church St.
62 B1 Churchill Dr.
61 A3 Circus Dr.
61 A3 Circus Pl.
61 A3 Circus Pl. La.
Circus Pl.
58 A1 Clachan Dr.
Skipness Dr.
64 A2 Claddens Quad.
64 A1 Claddens St.
63 C4 Clairmont Gdns.
65 C4 Clare St.
63 C4 Claremont Pl.
Claremont Ter.
59 A4 Claremont St.
63 C4 Claremont Ter.
63 C4 Claremont Ter. La.
Clifton St.
62 B2 Clarence Dr.
62 B2 Clarence Gdns.
64 C1 Clarendon La.
Clarendon St.
64 C1 Clarendon Pl.
64 C1 Clarendon St.
59 B4 Clark St.
Tower St.
63 C3 Clayslaps Rd.
Argyle St.
61 B3 Claythorn Av.
61 B3 Claythorn Circ.
Claythorn Av.
61 B3 Claythorn Ct.
Claythorn Pk.
61 B3 Claythorn Pk.
61 B3 Claythorn St.
61 B3 Claythorn Ter.
Claythorn Pk.
61 A3 Clayton Ter.
64 B1 Cleghorn St.
60 B2 Cleland La.
Cleland St.
60 B2 Cleland St.
62 A2 Cleveden Cres.
62 A2 Cleveden Cres. La.
Cleveden Dr.
62 A2 Cleveden Dr.
63 A3 Cleveden Gdns.
62 A2 Cleveden Pl.
62 A2 Cleveden Rd.
59 A4 Cleveland St.
63 C4 Cliff Rd.
58 B2 Clifford Gdns.
59 B3 Clifford La.
Gower St.
59 B3 Clifford Pl.
Clifford St.
58 B2 Clifford St.
63 C4 Clifton Pl.
Clifton St.
63 C4 Clifton St.
57 B3 Clincart Rd.
64 A2 Closeburn St.
63 B4 Clouston Ct.
63 B3 Clouston La.
Clouston St.
63 B3 Clouston St.
65 C4 Cloverbank St.
58 C1 Clunie Rd.
62 B1 Cluny Gdns.
59 B4 Clutha St.
Paisley Rd. W.
60 B1 Clyde Pl.
60 B1 Clyde St.
62 C1 Clyde Tunnel
58 A2 Clydebrae St.
63 C3 Clydeside
Expressway
62 C2 Clydeview
Dumbarton Rd.
62 C1 Clydeview La.
Broomhill Ter.
61 C3 Clydeview Ter.
Newhall St.
58 B2 Clynder St.
61 B4 Coalhill St.
65 C3 Cobden Rd.
60 B1 Coburg St.
60 A2 Cochrane St.
65 B4 Cockmuir St.
56 C1 Cogan Rd.
56 B1 Cogan St.
61 C3 Colbert St.
62 A2 Colchester Dr.
64 B2 Coldstream Pl.
Keppochhill Rd.
63 B4 Colebrooke La.
Colebrooke St.
63 B4 Colebrooke Pl.
Belmont St.
63 B4 Colebrooke St.
63 B4 Colebrooke Ter.
Colebrooke St.
64 A1 Colgrain St.
65 C4 Coll Pl.
65 C4 Coll St.
60 B2 College La.
High St.
60 A2 College St.
63 A3 Collina St.
61 A3 Collins St.
58 B1 Colonsay Rd.
64 A1 Coltmuir St.
58 A2 Columba St.
61 C3 Colvend St.
61 B4 Comely Pk. St.
61 B4 Comley Pl.
Gallowgate
60 B1 Commerce St.
60 B2 Commercial Ct.
60 C2 Commercial Rd.
59 A4 Congress Rd.
61 C4 Connal St.
63 A3 Contin Pl.
60 B1 Cook St.
63 C3 Coopers Well La.
Dumbarton Rd.
63 C3 Coopers Well St.
Dumbarton Rd.
58 B2 Copland Pl.
58 B2 Copland Quad.
58 B2 Copland Rd.
60 C1 Coplaw St.
57 B3 Cordiner St.
58 C1 Corkerhill Gdns.
64 C1 Corn St.
65 A4 Cornhill St.
59 B3 Cornwall St.
56 B1 Corrour Rd.
59 A4 Corunna St.
61 B3 Coulters La.
64 C2 Couper St.
57 C3 Courthill Av.
56 B1 Coustonhill St.
Pleasance St.
56 B1 Coustonholm Rd.
61 A4 Coventry Dr.
63 C4 Cowan La.
Cowan St.
63 C4 Cowan St.
64 C1 Cowcaddens Rd.
59 B4 Cowie St.
65 B3 Cowlairs Rd.
64 B2 Coxhill St.
56 C2 Coylton Rd.
57 C3 Craig Rd.
56 C1 Craiganour La.
56 C1 Craiganour Pl.
64 B2 Craigbank St.
56 C1 Craigellan Rd.
65 B4 Craigenbay St.
62 A1 Craigend Pl.
62 A1 Craigend St.
64 C1 Craighall Rd.
57 A3 Craigie St.
59 B3 Craigiehall Pl.
59 B4 Craigiehall St.
Craigiehall Pl.
61 A4 Craigielea St.
59 A4 Craigmaddie Ter.
La.
Derby St.
57 B3 Craigmillar Rd.
63 A4 Craigmont Dr.
63 A4 Craigmont St.
61 B3 Craignestock Pl.
London Rd.
61 B3 Craignestock St.
62 C2 Craignethan Gdns.
Lawrie St.
61 A4 Craigpark
61 A4 Craigpark Dr.
61 A4 Craigpark Ter.
Craigpark
58 B1 Craigton Dr.
58 B1 Craigton Pl.
Craigton Dr.
58 B1 Craigton Rd.
57 A4 Cramond St.
62 A2 Cranborne Rd.
59 A4 Cranston St.
63 B3 Cranworth La.
Great George St.
63 B3 Cranworth St.
62 C2 Crathie Dr.
62 C2 Crathie La.
Exeter Dr.
62 C2 Crawford La.
62 C2 Crawford Path
Crawford St.
62 C2 Crawford St.
61 B3 Creran St.
Tobago St.
63 B3 Cresswell La.
Great George St.
63 B3 Cresswell St.
58 A1 Cressy St.
65 B3 Crichton Pl.
Crichton St.
65 B3 Crichton St.
59 A4 Crieff Ct.
North St.
60 A1 Crimea St.
61 A4 Crinan St.
65 B3 Croftbank St.
57 C4 Crofthill Rd.
56 C2 Cromarty Av.
58 B1 Cromdale St.
63 A4 Cromer St.
57 C3 Crompton Av.
64 C1 Cromwell La.
Cromwell St.
64 C1 Cromwell St.
60 B2 Cross, The
57 A4 Crossbank Rd.
57 A4 Crossbank Ter.
57 A3 Crosshill Av.
58 B1 Crosslee St.
58 A1 Crossloan Pl.
58 A1 Crossloan Rd.
58 A1 Crossloan Ter.
56 A1 Crossmyloof
Gdns.
62 A1 Crow La.
62 B1 Crow Rd.
64 A2 Crowhill St.
62 B2 Crown Circ.
Crown Rd. S.
60 A2 Crown Ct.
Virginia St.
62 B2 Crown Gdns.
Crown Rd. N.
62 B2 Crown Mans.
North Gardner St.
62 B2 Crown Rd. N.
62 B2 Crown Rd. S.
60 C2 Crown St.
62 B2 Crown Ter.
Crown Rd. S.
61 B3 Crownpoint Rd.
61 B4 Crowpoint Rd.
Alma St.
58 B1 Cruden St.
61 B3 Cubie St.
61 A4 Culloden St.
Coventry Dr.
58 B1 Cults St.
60 B2 Cumberland Ct.
Gallowgate
60 C1 Cumberland La.
Cumberland St.
60 C2 Cumberland Pl.
60 B1 Cumberland St.
57 B3 Cumming Dr.
62 C1 Curle St.
57 B4 Curling Cres.
63 A4 Currie St.
57 B4 Curtis Av.
63 A4 Curzon St.
60 A2 Custom Ho. Quay
57 A3 Cuthbertson St.
64 A2 Cypress St.

D

57 A3 Daisy St.
63 C3 Dalcross La.
Byres Rd.
63 C3 Dalcross St.
61 C3 Dale Path
61 C3 Dale St.
62 A2 Daleview Av.
64 C1 Dalhousie La.
Scott St.
64 C1 Dalhousie La. W.
Buccleuch St.
64 C1 Dalhousie St.
60 B1 Dalintober St.
58 C2 Dalkeith Av.
63 B4 Dalmally St.
61 C4 Dalmarnock Ct.
Baltic St.
61 C3 Dalmarnock Rd.
63 C3 Dalnair St.
61 B4 Dalserf St.
59 C3 Dalziel Dr.
59 C3 Dalziel Quad.
Dalziel Dr.
58 C2 Dargarvel Av.
65 B4 Darnick St.
Hobden St.
56 A2 Darnley Gdns.
56 A2 Darnley Pl.
Darnley Rd.
56 A2 Darnley Rd.
56 A2 Darnley St.
64 B1 Dartford St.
58 A2 Dava St.
61 C4 Davaar St.
62 A2 Daventry Dr.
61 B4 David St.
64 B1 Dawson Pl.
Dawson Rd.
64 B1 Dawson Rd.
60 A2 Deanside La.
Rottenrow
56 B2 Deanston Dr.
62 A1 Debdale Cotts.
Whittingehame
Dr.
57 C3 Delvin Rd.
64 B1 Denham St.
64 B2 Denmark St.
59 A4 Derby St.
59 A4 Derby Ter. La.
Derby St.
64 B1 Derwent St.
62 B2 Devon Gdns.
Hyndland Rd.
60 C1 Devon Pl.
60 C1 Devon St.
62 B2 Devonshire
Gdns.
62 B2 Devonshire
Gdns. La.
Hyndland Rd.
62 B2 Devonshire Ter.
62 B2 Devonshire Ter.
La.
Hughenden Rd.
63 B4 Dick St.
Henderson St.
62 C1 Dilwara Av.
59 A3 Dingwall St.
Kelvinhaugh St.
56 A2 Dinmont Pl.
Norham St.
56 A1 Dinmont Rd.
56 B2 Dirleton Av.
57 A3 Dixon Av.
57 A4 Dixon Rd.
60 B1 Dixon St.
64 C1 Dobbies Ln.
60 A2 Dobbies Ln. Pl.
56 A1 Dolphin Rd.
64 B1 Doncaster St.
56 C1 Doonfoot Rd.
61 C4 Dora St.
62 A2 Dorchester Av.
62 A2 Dorchester Ct.
Dorchester Av.
62 A2 Dorchester Pl.
61 B3 Dornoch St.
59 A4 Dorset Sq.
Dorset St.
59 A4 Dorset St.
60 A1 Douglas La.
West George St.
60 A1 Douglas St.
59 C4 Douglas Ter.
Shields Rd.
63 B4 Doune Gdns.
63 B4 Doune Quad.
56 B1 Dovecot
Shawhill Rd.
59 A4 Dover St.
63 C3 Dowanhill Pl.
Old Dumbarton
Rd.
63 C3 Dowanhill St.
63 B3 Dowanside La.
Byres Rd.
63 B3 Dowanside Rd.
62 C2 Dowanvale Ter.
White St.
65 B3 Downs St.
64 B1 Dows Pl.
Possil Rd.
61 B3 Drake St.
62 C2 Drem Pl.
Merkland St.
58 A1 Drive Rd.
65 A4 Drumbottie Rd.
62 A1 Drummond Gdns.
Crow Rd.
58 A1 Drumoyne Av.
58 B1 Drumoyne Circ.
58 A1 Drumoyne Dr.
58 B1 Drumoyne Pl.
Drumoyne Circ.
58 B1 Drumoyne Quad.
58 B1 Drumoyne Rd.
58 A1 Drumoyne Sq.
60 A1 Drury St.
63 B4 Dryburgh Gdns.
61 A3 Drygate
58 B1 Drymen St.
Morven St.
62 B2 Dudley Dr.
61 A3 Duke St.
62 C2 Dumbarton Rd.
58 C2 Dumbreck Av.
58 C2 Dumbreck Ct.
58 C2 Dumbreck Rd.
58 C2 Dumbreck Sq.
Dumbreck Av.
63 B4 Dunard St.
63 C3 Dunaskin St.
63 A3 Dunbeith Pl.
64 C1 Dunblane St.
61 A3 Dunchattan Pl.
Duke St.
61 A3 Dunchattan St.
60 A2 Dundas La.
60 A2 Dundas St.
64 C1 Dundasvale Ct.
Maitland St.
64 C1 Dundasvale Rd.
Maitland St.
63 B3 Dundonald Rd.
56 B2 Dundrennan Rd.
63 C4 Dunearn St.
58 B1 Dunellan St.
60 B2 Dunlop St.
60 B1 Dunmore La.
Norfolk St.
60 B1 Dunmore St.
61 C4 Dunn St.
65 C4 Dunolly St.
61 B4 Dunrobin St.
58 A2 Dunsmuir St.
65 B3 Duntocher St.
Northcroft Rd.
61 A4 Duntroon St.
59 B3 Durham St.
56 A1 Durward Av.
56 A1 Durwood Ct.
62 C2 Dyce La.
60 B2 Dyers La.
Turnbull St.
65 B4 Dykemuir Pl.
65 B4 Dykemuir Quad.
Dykemuir St.
65 B4 Dykemuir St.

E

64 C2 Eagle St.
59 B4 Eaglesham Ct.
Blackburn St.
59 B4 Eaglesham Pl.
56 B2 Earlspark Av.
60 A1 East Bath La.
Sauchiehall St.
61 B3 East Campbell St.
65 A4 Eastburn Rd.
62 B1 Eastcote Av.
65 B4 Eastcroft Ter.
61 A4 Eastercraigs
65 B3 Eastfield Rd.
59 A3 Eastvale Pl.
56 B1 Eastwood Av.
65 A3 Eccles St.
64 A2 Eday St.
62 C2 Edelweiss Ter.
Gardner St.
65 B3 Edgefauld Av.
65 B3 Edgefauld Dr.
65 A3 Edgefauld Pl.
Balgrayhill Rd.
65 B3 Edgefauld Rd.
62 B2 Edgehill La.
Marlborough Av.
62 B2 Edgehill Rd.

56 B2 Edgemont St.
64 C1 Edington St.
58 B1 Edmiston Dr.
59 A3 Edward St.
  Lumsden St.
59 B3 Edwin St.
60 B1 Eglinton Ct.
60 C1 Eglinton La.
  Eglinton St.
60 C1 Eglinton St.
61 B3 Elcho St.
58 A1 Elder St.
58 A1 Elderpark Gdns.
58 A1 Elderpark Gro.
58 A1 Elderpark St.
63 C4 Elderslie St.
63 C4 Eldon St.
62 C2 Eldon Ter.
  Caird Dr.
61 B4 Elgin St.
63 C3 Elie St.
59 B3 Elizabeth St.
56 B1 Ellangowan Rd.
64 B1 Ellesmere St.
59 A4 Elliot St.
  Elliot St.
59 A4 Elliot Pl.
59 A4 Elliot St.
56 C1 Ellisland Rd.
60 A1 Elmbank Cres.
  Elmbank St.
59 A4 Elmbank La.
  North St.
60 A1 Elmbank St.
59 A4 Elmbank St. La.
  North St.
57 A4 Elmfoot St.
57 C3 Elmore Av.
57 C3 Elmore La.
65 B3 Elmvale Row
65 B3 Elmvale Row E.
  Elmvale Row
65 B3 Elmvale Row W.
  Elmvale Row
65 A3 Elmvale St.
62 B1 Elmwood Av.
62 B1 Elmwood Gdns.
  Randolph Rd.
62 B1 Elmwood La.
  Elmwood Av.
62 B1 Elmwood Ter.
  Crow Rd.
59 A3 Elphinstone Pl.
57 C3 Elrig Rd.
64 B1 Eltham St.
64 A1 Emerson St.
61 B3 Emily Pl.
62 A2 Endfield Av.
64 B2 Endrick St.
62 B2 Endsleigh Gdns.
  Partickhill Rd.
56 C1 Ericht Rd.
60 C2 Errol Gdns.
58 C2 Erskine Av.
57 C2 Eskdale St.
63 C3 Esmond St.
62 B1 Essex Dr.
62 B1 Essex La.
63 C4 Eton Gdns.
  Oakfield Av.
63 C4 Eton La.
  Great George St.
63 C4 Eton Pl.
  Oakfield Av.
63 C4 Eton Ter.
  Oakfield Av.
56 B1 Ettrick Pl.
59 A3 Ewart Pl.
  Kelvinhaugh St.
60 A2 Exchange Pl.
  Buchanan St.
62 C2 Exeter Dr.
62 C2 Exeter La.
  Exeter Dr.
59 A4 Exhibition Way

F

61 C4 Fairbairn Path
  Ruby St.
61 C4 Fairbairn St.
  Dalmarnock Rd.
57 C4 Fairfax Av.
58 A1 Fairfield Gdns.
58 A1 Fairfield Pl.
58 A1 Fairfield St.
58 B2 Fairley St.
62 C2 Fairlie Pk. Dr.

60 C1 Falfield St.
62 B2 Falkland Mans.
  Clarence Dr.
62 B2 Falkland St.
57 B3 Falloch Rd.
58 C2 Farm Rd.
64 C1 Farnell St.
60 C2 Fauldhouse St.
63 B4 Fergus Ct.
63 B4 Fergus Dr.
65 A3 Fernbank St.
57 C4 Ferncroft Dr.
62 A2 Ferngrove Av.
56 C1 Fernleigh Rd.
58 A2 Ferry Rd.
62 C1 Ferryden St.
56 C1 Fersit St.
57 C4 Fetlar Dr.
61 B4 Fielden St.
61 B4 Fielden St.
62 A1 Fifth Av.
64 B2 Finlas St.
61 A4 Finlay Dr.
61 C3 Finnart Sq.
61 C3 Finnart St.
58 B1 Finsbay St.
57 B4 Fintry Dr.
64 B1 Firhill Rd.
64 B1 Firhill St.
61 A3 Firpark Pl.
  Firpark St.
61 A3 Firpark St.
61 A3 Firpark Ter.
  Ark La.
58 C2 First Gdns.
57 C4 Firwood Dr.
61 A3 Fisher Ct.
59 A4 Fitzroy La.
  North Claremont St.
59 A4 Fitzroy Pl.
  North Claremont St.
61 B4 Fleming St.
65 B4 Flemington St.
58 C2 Fleurs Av.
58 C2 Fleurs Rd.
60 B2 Florence St.
61 C4 Florentine Pl.
  Gibson St.
63 C4 Florentine Ter.
  Southpark Av.
57 B3 Florida Av.
57 B3 Florida Cres.
57 B3 Florida Dr.
57 B3 Florida Sq.
57 B3 Florida St.
61 B3 Fogo Pl.
61 B3 Forbes Dr.
61 B3 Forbes St.
63 B3 Ford Rd.
61 B4 Fordneuk St.
62 C2 Fordyce St.
65 B4 Foresthall Cres.
65 B4 Foresthall Dr.
65 C4 Forge Pl.
65 C4 Forge St.
61 B4 Forrest St.
65 C4 Forrestfield St.
59 C4 Forth St.
63 A3 Fortingall Av.
  Grandtully Dr.
63 A3 Fortingall Pl.
56 C2 Fortrose St.
56 A1 Fotheringay La.
  Beaton Rd.
56 A1 Fotheringay Rd.
62 A1 Foulis La.
62 A1 Foulis St.
61 B4 Foundary St.
61 B4 Foundry Open
61 B3 Fountain St.
64 C2 Fountainwell Av.
64 C2 Fountainwell Pl.
64 C2 Fountainwell Rd.
64 C2 Fountainwell Rd.
65 C3 Fountainwell Ter.
60 B2 Fourth Gdns.
60 B2 Fox La.
60 B1 Fox St.
60 C1 Francis St.
56 A2 Frankfort St.

61 C3 Franklin St.
64 B2 Fraserbank St.
  Keppochhill Rd.
61 B4 Frazer St.
61 B4 French St.
56 C2 Friarton Rd.
64 B2 Fruin Pl.
64 B2 Fruin St.

G

64 A2 Gadlock St.
65 C3 Gadshill St.
61 C4 Gailes St.
63 A3 Gairbraid Av.
63 A3 Gairbraid Ct.
63 A3 Gairbraid Pl.
62 C2 Gairn St.
  Castlebank St.
58 A1 Galbraith Av.
  Burghead Dr.
65 A3 Galloway St.
60 B2 Gallowgate
62 C2 Gardner St.
61 B4 Garfield St.
58 A1 Garmouth Ct.
  Garmouth St.
58 A1 Garmouth Gdns.
58 A1 Garmouth St.
64 C1 Garnet La.
  Garnet St.
64 C1 Garnet St.
64 C1 Garnethill St.
65 C3 Garnkirk St.
65 C3 Garnock St.
63 A3 Garrioch Cres.
63 A3 Garrioch Dr.
63 A3 Garrioch Gate
63 A3 Garrioch Quad.
63 B3 Garrioch Rd.
63 B4 Garriochmill Rd.
  Raeberry St.
63 B4 Garriochmill Way
  Woodside Rd.
57 B3 Garry St.
64 B1 Garscube Rd.
65 B4 Gartferry St.
60 A3 Garth St.
61 A4 Garthland Dr.
61 A4 Gartness St.
63 B4 Gartochmill Rd.
57 A3 Garturk St.
61 C4 Garvald Ct.
  Baltic St.
61 C4 Garvald St.
61 B4 Gateside St.
59 B4 General Terminus Quay
62 A1 George Reith Av.
60 A2 George Sq.
60 A2 George St.
65 C3 Gibb St.
  Royston Rd.
63 C3 Gibson St. (G12)
61 C3 Gibson St. (G40)
57 C3 Gilbert St.
61 B4 Gills Ct.
60 C2 Gilmour Pl.
64 C1 Gladstone St.
60 B1 Glasgow Bri.
60 B1 Glasgow Grn.
63 B4 Glasgow St.
56 C2 Glasserton Pl.
56 C2 Glasserton Rd.
60 A2 Glassford St.
60 A2 Glebe Ct.
64 C2 Glebe St.
59 C4 Glenapp St.
62 C2 Glenavon Ter.
  Crow Rd.
65 C3 Glenbarr St.
59 A3 Glencairn Dr.
56 A2 Glencairn Gdns.
  Glencairn Dr.
57 C4 Glencroft Rd.
61 B4 Glendale Pl.
  Glendale St.
61 B4 Glendale St.
62 C1 Glendore St.
64 C1 Glenfarg St.
63 A3 Glenfinnan Dr.
63 A3 Glenfinnan Pl.
63 A3 Glenfinnan Rd.
65 A2 Glenhead Cres.
64 A2 Glenhead St.
61 B4 Glenpark St.
57 A3 Glenpark Ter.

56 C1 Glenspean Pl.
  Glenspean St.
56 C1 Glenspean St.
60 B1 Gloucester St.
61 A4 Golfhill Dr.
61 A4 Golfhill La.
  Whitehill St.
61 A3 Golfhill Ter.
  Firpark St.
58 A2 Golspie St.
60 B2 Goosedubbs
  Stockwell St.
60 B2 Gorbals Cross
60 B1 Gorbals La.
  Oxford St.
60 B1 Gorbals St.
60 A1 Gordon La.
60 A1 Gordon St.
63 A3 Gorstan Pl.
  Wyndford Rd.
64 B2 Gourlay Path
  Endrick St.
65 B3 Gourlay St.
  Crichton St.
60 C1 Gourock St.
58 A2 Govan Cross
58 A1 Govan Rd.
59 B3 Govanhill St.
59 B3 Gower St.
59 C3 Gower St.
59 B3 Gower Ter.
59 A4 Grace St.
63 A4 Grafton Pl.
61 B3 Graham Sq.
63 B3 Granby La.
  Great George St.
63 B3 Granby Pl.
  Great George St.
63 A3 Grandtully Dr.
57 B3 Grange Rd.
63 C4 Grant St.
59 B3 Grantley Gdns.
59 B3 Grantley St.
59 C3 Granville St.
60 B2 Great Dovehill
63 B3 Great George La.
  Great George St.
63 B3 Great George St.
63 B3 Great Kelvin La.
  Glasgow St.
62 A2 Great Western Rd.
63 B3 Great Western Ter.
61 C3 Green, The
61 C3 Green Lo. Ter.
  Greenhead St.
61 B3 Green St.
60 B2 Greendyke St.
58 A1 Greenfield St.
61 C3 Greenhead St.
57 C3 Greenholme St.
  Holmlea Rd.
62 A1 Greenlea St.
57 C3 Greenock Av.
56 B1 Greenview St.
58 A2 Greenwell Pl.
58 A1 Greenwell St.
  Govan Rd.
61 C4 Gretna St.
63 B3 Grosvenor Cres.
  Observatory Rd.
63 B3 Grosvenor Cres. La.
  Observatory Rd.
63 B3 Grosvenor La.
  Byres Rd.
63 B3 Grosvenor Mans.
  Observatory Rd.
64 C2 Grosvenor Ter.
57 C4 Grovepark Ct.
64 C1 Grovepark Gdns.
64 C1 Grovepark Pl.
64 B1 Grovepark St.
61 C3 Gryffe St.
62 C2 Gullane St.
  Purdon St.
63 A3 Guthrie St.

H

56 A1 Haggs Rd.
65 B4 Haig St.
57 A3 Hairmyres St.
  Govanhill St.

56 A2 Halbert St.
60 C2 Hallside St.
58 C2 Hamilton Av.
63 B4 Hamilton Dr.
63 B4 Hamilton Pk. Av.
57 A4 Hamilton St.
64 B1 Hamiltonhill Cres.
  Hamiltonhill Rd.
64 B1 Hamiltonhill Rd.
57 B3 Hampden Dr.
  Cathcart Rd.
57 B3 Hampden La.
  Cathcart Rd.
57 B3 Hampden Ter.
  Cathcart Rd.
57 B4 Hangingshaw Pl.
60 A2 Hanover St.
61 A4 Harcourt Dr.
58 A1 Harhill St.
59 B3 Harley St.
64 A2 Harmetray St.
58 A2 Harmony Pl.
58 A2 Harmony Row
58 A2 Harmony Sq.
62 C1 Harmsworth St.
63 A4 Harrison Dr.
58 A1 Harvey St.
59 B3 Harvie St.
63 C3 Hastie St.
  Old Dumbarton Rd.
62 A1 Hatfield Dr.
63 A4 Hathaway La.
  Avenuepark St.
63 A4 Hathaway St.
61 C3 Hatters Row
  Dalmarnock Rd.
63 A3 Haugh Rd.
63 C3 Havelock La.
  Dowanhill St.
63 C3 Havelock St.
64 A2 Hawthorn Quad.
64 A2 Hawthorn St.
62 C2 Hayburn Ct.
62 B2 Hayburn Cres.
62 B2 Hayburn La.
  Queensborough Gdns.
62 C2 Hayburn St.
60 C2 Hayfield St.
62 C2 Haylynn St.
64 A1 Hayston Cres.
64 A1 Hayston St.
64 A1 Haywood St.
59 C3 Hazelwood Rd.
64 A1 Hazlitt St.
59 B4 Heather St.
  Scotland St.
56 B1 Hector Rd.
61 A3 Heddle Pl.
  Cadogan St.
58 B1 Helen St.
63 B4 Henderson St.
63 B4 Herbert St.
60 B1 Herbertson St.
  Eglinton St.
61 C3 Heron St.
56 A1 Herries Rd.
59 C4 Herriet St.
62 A1 Herschell St.
  Foulis La.
62 A2 Hertford Av.
64 A1 Hexham Gdns.
59 A3 Hickman St.
57 A3 Hickory St.
64 C1 High Craighall Rd.
60 B2 High St.
63 C3 Highburgh Rd.
63 B3 Highburgh Ter.
  Highburgh Rd.
57 C4 Highcroft Av.
62 A2 Highfield Dr.
62 A2 Highfield Pl.
59 A3 Highland La.
64 C1 Hill St.
61 A4 Hillfoot St.
63 C3 Hillhead Gdns.
  Hillhead St.
63 C4 Hillhead Pl.
  Bank St.
63 B3 Hillhead St.
63 B3 Hillhouse St.
65 B3 Hillkirk Pl.
65 B3 Hillkirk St.

65 B3 Hillkirk St. La.
  Hillkirk St.
56 C1 Hillpark Dr.
63 C3 Hillsborough Sq.
  Hillhead St.
63 B4 Hillsborough Ter.
  Bower St.
62 B2 Hillside Gdns.
  Turnberry Rd.
62 B2 Hillside Gdns. La.
  North Gardner St.
64 B1 Hinshaw St.
58 B2 Hinshelwood Dr.
58 B2 Hinshelwood Pl.
  Edmiston Dr.
64 B1 Hobart St.
65 B4 Hobden St.
59 A3 Hoey St.
56 C1 Holeburn Rd.
60 A1 Holland St.
65 B4 Holly Dr.
65 C4 Hollybank St.
57 A3 Hollybrook St.
60 A1 Holm St.
56 B1 Holmbank Av.
62 C1 Holmfauld Rd.
58 A1 Holmfaulddhead Dr.
58 A1 Holmfaulddhead Pl.
  Govan Rd.
57 C3 Holmhead Cres.
57 C3 Holmhead Pl.
57 B3 Holmlea Rd.
63 C4 Holyrood Cres.
63 C4 Holyrood Quad.
61 B4 Holywell St.
60 A1 Hope St.
63 A3 Hopefield Av.
64 B1 Hopehill Pl.
  Hopehill Rd.
64 B1 Hopehill Rd.
65 B4 Hopetoun Ter.
  Foresthall Dr.
65 A3 Horne St.
  Hawthorn St.
65 B4 Hornshill St.
63 B3 Horslethill Rd.
60 C1 Hospital St.
63 B4 Hotspur St.
59 A4 Houldsworth La.
  Finnieston St.
59 A4 Houldsworth St.
59 B4 Houston Pl.
59 B4 Houston St.
60 B1 Howard St.
58 A2 Howat St.
59 B4 Howwood St.
61 C3 Hozier St.
62 C2 Hubbard Dr.
62 B2 Hughenden Dr.
62 B2 Hughenden Gdns.
62 B2 Hughenden La.
62 B2 Hughenden Rd.
  Hughenden Rd.
63 A4 Hugo St.
61 B3 Hunter St.
65 A3 Huntershill St.
65 C3 Huntingdon Rd.
65 C3 Huntingdon Sq.
  Huntingdon Rd.
63 B3 Huntly Gdns.
63 B3 Huntly Rd.
60 A2 Hutcheson St.
60 A1 Hutchinson Ct.
  Hope St.
58 A1 Hutton Dr.
65 A3 Huxley St.
65 A3 Hydepark Pl.
  Springburn Rd.
59 A4 Hydepark St.
58 A2 Hyndford St.
62 C2 Hyndland Av.
62 C2 Hyndland Rd.
63 C3 Hyndland St.

I

59 B3 Ibrox St.
58 B2 Ibrox Ter.
58 B2 Ibrox Ter. La.
58 B3 Ibroxholm La.
  Paisley Rd. W.
58 B2 Ibroxholm Oval
58 B2 Ibroxholm Pl.
62 C1 Inchfad Dr.
62 C1 Inchlee St.
60 A1 India St.

	Street	Pg/Ref
A4	Ingleby Dr.	56 B1
A3	Inglefield St.	59 C4
B4	Inglis St.	58 A1
A2	Ingram St.	60 A2
B1	Inverclyde Gdns.	65 C4
	Broomhill Dr.	62 C1
B2	Invergordon Av.	62 C1
B2	Inverkip St.	
	Thornwood Dr.	
A3	Inverlair Av.	61 A4
	Wyndford Rd.	
B2	Inverurie St.	63 B3
A2	Iona Ct.	59 A4
A2	Iona St.	61 B3
C4	Irvine St.	64 B2
B2	Iser La.	64 B2
		57 B4

J

	Street	Pg/Ref
B1	Jamaica St.	57 B4
B2	James Gray St.	
B2	James Morrison St.	61 C4
	St. Andrews Sq.	63 B3
C3	James Nisbet St.	
C3	James St.	63 B3
A1	James Watt La.	64 B1
	James Watt St.	64 B1
A1	James Watt St.	63 B3
A3	Jamieson Ct.	
A3	Jamieson Path	63 B3
	Jamieson St.	
A3	Jamieson St.	63 B3
B4	Janefield St.	59 B4
B4	Jardine St.	60 C2
A2	Jasgray St.	60 B1
B4	Jedburgh Gdns.	
A1	Jessie St.	65 C4
B2	Jocelyn Sq.	60 C1
A3	John Knox La.	
	Drygate	57 B4
A2	John Knox St.	57 C3
A2	John St.	57 C3
B1	Johnshaven St.	62 C2
	Bengal St.	58 B2
A1	Jordanhill La.	
	Copland Rd.	
B3	Julian Av.	
	Julian Av.	56 A2
B3	Julian La.	64 B1
	Julian Av.	
B1	Jura Ct.	56 A1
B1	Jura St.	57 C3
		63 A3

K

	Street	Pg/Ref
C1	Kames St.	56 C1
C1	Karol Path	58 B1
	St. Peters St.	57 C3
B3	Kay St.	64 B2
C4	Keir St.	58 B2
C3	Keith Ct.	
	Keith St.	62 A1
C3	Keith St.	60 B1
B4	Kelbourne St.	60 C2
C2	Kellas St.	60 C2
B1	Kelty Pl.	
	Bedford St.	57 C3
C1	Kelty St.	57 A3
	Eglinton St.	
A1	Kelvin Ct.	61 A3
B1	Kelvin Dr.	57 B3
C3	Kelvin Way	57 B4
C3	Kelvindale Bldgs.	57 B3
	Kelvindale Rd.	62 B2
A3	Kelvindale Cotts.	
	Kelvindale Rd.	
A3	Kelvindale Gdns.	62 B2
	Kelvindale Rd.	
A3	Kelvindale Glen	
	Kelvindale Rd.	62 B2
A3	Kelvindale Pl.	
A3	Kelvindale Rd.	57 B4
A4	Kelvingrove St.	57 C4
A4	Kelvingrove Ter.	57 C4
	Kelvingrove St.	
A3	Kelvinhaugh Pl.	57 C4
	Kelvinhaugh St.	
A3	Kelvinhaugh St.	57 C4
B4	Kelvinside Av.	57 B4
	Queen Margaret Dr.	
B4	Kelvinside Dr.	57 A3
B4	Kelvinside Gdns.	57 B4
B4	Kelvinside Gdns. E.	57 C4
B4	Kelvinside Ter. S.	
B4	Kelvinside Ter. W.	59 B4
B3	Kemp St.	60 B1
B2	Kendal Av.	
A2	Kendal Dr.	57 C4
B3	Kendal Ter.	57 B3

Street	Pg/Ref
Kenilworth Av.	57 B3
Kenmure St.	59 C4
Kennedar Dr.	61 C4
Kennedy St.	59 B4
Kennet St.	63 B3
Kennoway Dr.	
Thornwood Dr.	
Kennoway La.	56 C2
Kennyhill Sq.	65 C4
Kensington Gate	64 A2
Kensington Rd.	
Kensington Rd.	56 B1
Kent Rd.	56 A1
Kent St.	58 C1
Keppoch St.	63 A3
Keppochhill Rd.	63 A3
Kerr St.	63 B4
Kerrycroy Av.	63 B3
Kerrycroy Pl.	63 A3
Kerrycroy Av.	
Kerrycroy St.	63 A3
Kerrydale St.	
Kerrydale St.	61 C4
Kersland La.	63 B3
Kersland St.	63 B3
Kessock Dr.	64 B1
Kessock Pl.	64 B1
Kew Gdns.	63 B3
Ruthven St.	
Kew La.	63 B3
Saltoun St.	56 C1
Kew Ter.	61 B4
Keyden St.	57 C3
Kidston St.	59 B3
Kilbarchan St.	57 B3
Bedford St.	57 B3
Kilberry St.	
Kilbirnie St.	59 C4
Kilbride St.	
Kilchattan Dr.	59 C4
Kildary Av.	64 C2
Kildary Rd.	
Kildonan Dr.	
Kildonan Ter.	63 C4
Copland Rd.	63 B4
Kildrostan St.	59 C3
Terregles Av.	58 C1
Kilearn St.	61 A3
Killermont St.	56 C2
Killiegrew Rd.	60 B1
Kilmailing Rd.	63 B3
Kilmair Pl.	64 A1
Wyndford Rd.	59 B3
Kilmarnock Rd.	65 A4
Kilmaurs St.	58 B1
Kinalty Rd.	63 B3
Kinbuck St.	62 A2
Kinfauns Ter.	
Copland Rd.	
King Edward Rd.	63 B3
King George V Bri.	
King St.	63 B3
King's Bri.	63 B3
King's Dr.	
King's Pk. Av.	
Kingarth St.	59 A4
Kinghorn Dr.	59 A4
Kings Cross	
Kings Pk. Rd.	61 C3
Kingsacre Rd.	60 C1
Kingsbarns Dr.	
Eglinton St.	58 A1
Kingsborough Gdns.	65 B4
Kingsborough Gate	59 B3
Prince Albert Rd.	
Kingsborough Ter.	57 B3
Hyndland Rd.	57 A3
Kingsbrae Av.	56 B2
Kingsbridge Cres.	57 B3
Kingsbridge Dr.	63 C4
Kingscliffe Av.	57 B3
Kingscourt Av.	57 B4
Kingsdale Av.	57 B4
Kingsdyke Av.	57 B4
Kingshill Dr.	58 C2
Kingshouse Av.	56 C2
Kingshurst Av.	58 A1
Kingsley Av.	61 A4
Kingslynn Dr.	57 A3
Kingslynn La.	
Kingslynn Dr.	57 B4
Kingston Bri.	63 A3
Kingston St.	
Kingswood Dr.	60 C1
Kingussie St.	57 C4
Kinmount Av.	62 B2

Street	Pg/Ref
Kinmount La.	62 C2
Kinmount Av.	62 C2
Kinnear Rd.	59 B3
Kinning St.	
Kinnoul La.	60 B2
Downhill St.	65 B3
Kintore Rd.	61 B4
Kintra St.	60 C2
Kintyre St.	60 C2
Kippen St.	64 A2
Kirk La.	56 B1
Riverbank St.	
Kirkcaldy Rd.	56 A1
Kirkdale Dr.	58 C1
Kirkhill Dr.	63 C3
Kirkhill Pl.	62 C2
Kirkland St.	65 B3
Kirklee Circ.	
Kirklee Gdns.	56 B1
Kirklee Gdns. La.	56 C1
Kirklee Pl.	63 A3
Kirklee Quad.	63 B3
Kirklee Quad. La.	
Trongate	59 B4
Kirklee Rd.	
Kirklee Ter.	64 B1
Kirklee Ter. La.	65 A3
Kirklee Ter.	65 A3
Kirkoswald Rd.	65 A3
Kirkpatrick St.	65 A3
Kirkwell Rd.	64 C1
Kirkwood St.	57 C3
Knockhill Dr.	57 C3
Knockhill La.	56 A2
Mount Annan Dr.	59 C4
Knowehead Gdns.	56 C2
Knowehead Ter.	57 B3
Knowehead Ter.	56 B2
Kyle St.	58 B2

L

Street	Pg/Ref
La Belle Pl.	63 C4
La Crosse Ter.	63 B4
Laburnum Rd.	59 C3
Ladybank Dr.	58 C1
Ladywell St.	61 C4
Laggan Rd.	56 C2
Laidlaw St.	63 B3
Laird Pl.	
Lamb St.	63 B3
Lambhill St.	59 B3
Lamont Rd.	65 A4
Lanark St.	
Lancaster Cres.	57 B3
Lancaster Cres. La.	62 A2
Lancaster Ter.	63 B3
Westbourne Gdns. W.	57 C3
Lancaster Ter. La.	58 A1
Westbourne Gdns. W.	62 C1
Lancefield Quay	63 B4
Lancefield St.	59 A4
Landressy Pl.	59 A4
Landressy St.	
Langbank St.	60 C1
Eglinton St.	
Langlands Path	65 B3
Langrig Rd.	
Langshot St.	64 B2
Langside Av.	
Langside Gdns.	61 A4
Langside Pl.	56 C1
Langside Pl.	57 B3
Lansdowne Cres.	63 C4
Lansdowne Cres. La.	57 B3
Great Western Rd.	56 A2
Lanton Rd.	56 C2
Larch Rd.	65 C4
Largie Rd.	57 A4
Largo Pl.	58 A2
Largs St.	61 A4
Larkfield St.	57 A3
Cathcart Rd.	
Latherton Dr.	60 B2
Latherton Pl.	
Latherton Dr.	60 B2
Lauder St.	61 B3
Eglinton St.	
Lauderdale Gdns.	58 C1

Street	Pg/Ref
Laurel Pl.	59 B3
Laurel St.	63 B3
Laurieston La.	
Kensington Rd.	
Laurieston Rd.	63 B3
Laverockhall St.	63 B3
Law St.	
Lawmoor Av.	64 C2
Lawmoor La.	60 C1
Ballater St.	
Lawmoor Pl.	63 B3
Lawmoor Av.	58 A2
Lawmoor Rd.	57 B4
Lawmoor St.	57 B4
Lawrence St.	63 C3
Lawrie St.	58 C1
Leckethill St.	65 B3
Leckie St.	59 A3
Ledard Rd.	56 B2
Ledi Rd.	59 A3
Leicester Av.	58 A1
Leighton St.	58 A2
Leitchs Ct.	64 B2
Trongate	
Lendel Pl.	64 B2
Paisley Rd. W.	59 A3
Leny St.	63 B4
Lenzie Dr.	65 A3
Lenzie Pl.	65 A3
Lenzie St.	63 C4
Lenzie Ter.	65 A3
Lerwick St.	63 B3
Leslie Rd.	
Leslie St.	59 C4
Letham Ct.	56 C2
Letham Dr.	58 A2
Letherby Dr.	61 C3
Lethington Av.	64 B2
Lettoch St.	
Leven St.	59 C4
Leyden Ct.	63 A4
Leyden St.	
Leyden Gdns.	63 A4
Leyden St.	
Leyden St.	57 C3
Lily St.	61 C3
Lilybank Gdns.	
Madras St.	61 C3
Lilybank Gdns. La.	61 C3
Great George St.	58 B2
Lilybank Ter.	59 B4
Great George St.	64 C1
Lilybank Ter. La.	64 C1
Great George St.	63 A4
Lindores St.	64 B1
Somerville Dr.	61 B4
Lindsay Dr.	58 A1
Lindsay Pl.	56 C1
Linfern Rd.	56 C1
Linnwood Ct.	62 A2
Bowling Grn. Rd.	61 B4
Linthouse Bldgs.	
Holmfauld Rd.	56 B1
Linthouse Rd.	
Linwood Ter.	56 B1
Glasgow St.	62 B1
Lismore Rd.	57 C3
Lister St.	65 A3
Little Dovehill	63 C3
Little St.	59 A4
Littleinch St.	56 B2
Edgefauld Rd.	
Livingstone St.	
Keppochhill Rd.	
Lloyd St.	61 A4
Loanbank Quad.	58 A2
Lochburn Rd.	
Lochlea Rd.	56 A2
Lochleven La.	63 B3
Lochleven St.	58 C1
Lochside St.	60 A2
Minard Rd.	
Lockerbie Av.	59 B4
Lockhart St.	56 A2
Logan St.	56 A2
Logie St.	61 B3
Lomond St.	60 B1
London Arc.	
London Rd.	62 B1
London La.	62 B1
London Rd.	59 B4
London Rd.	
Seaward St.	
Loom St.	63 B4
Stevenson St.	61 A4
Lora Dr.	60 B2

Street	Pg/Ref
Lorne St.	60 A2
Lorraine Gdns.	61 C3
Kensington Rd.	
Lorraine Rd.	61 A4
Lothian Gdns.	64 C1
Loudon Ter.	63 B4
Observatory Rd.	58 B1
Lovat St.	58 B1
Lower English Bldgs.	56 A2
Masterton St.	64 B2
Lowther Ter.	60 C2
Luath St.	58 A2
Lubas Av.	57 B4
Lubas Pl.	57 B4
Lubnaig Rd.	60 C1
Lugar Dr.	61 C4
Luing Rd.	58 B1
Lumloch St.	64 B2
Lumsden La.	58 A2
Lumsden St.	
Lumsden St.	59 C4
Lunan Pl.	59 C3
Luss Rd.	59 C3
Lyall Pl.	59 C4
Keppochhill Rd.	59 C4
Lyall St.	60 C1
Lymburn St.	59 C4
Lyndhurst Gdns.	59 C4
Lynedoch Cres.	60 B2
Lynedoch Pl.	57 B3
Lynedoch St.	
Prospecthill Rd.	
Lynedoch Ter.	57 A3
Lynn Gdns.	
Great George St.	63 B3

M

Street	Pg/Ref
Macdougal St.	56 B1
Mackechnie St.	58 A2
Mackeith St.	60 A2
Borron St.	59 C4
Mackie St.	61 A3
Mackinlay St.	61 B3
Maclean St.	58 B1
Maclellan St.	61 A3
Madison Av.	
Madison La.	61 A3
Carmunnock Rd.	59 A4
Madras Pl.	
Madras St.	57 B3
Madras St.	61 B3
Mafeking St.	58 B2
Main St.	60 A2
Mair St.	64 C1
Maitland St.	
Dunblane St.	
Malloch St.	60 B2
Maltbarns St.	
High St.	
Malvern Ct.	62 C2
Mambeg Dr.	61 A4
Mamore Pl.	62 C1
Mamore St.	56 C1
Manchester Dr.	62 C2
Manitoba Pl.	61 C3
Janefield St.	
Mannering Ct.	61 C3
Mannering Rd.	58 A1
Pollokshaws Rd.	61 B3
Manor Rd.	58 A1
Manse Brae	57 C3
Mansel St.	65 A3
Mansfield St.	64 C1
Mansion St.	
Mansionhouse Gdns.	63 A3
Mansionhouse Rd.	
Mansionhouse Rd.	59 C4
Maple Rd.	65 A3
March La.	57 C3
March St.	65 A4
Marchmont Ter.	65 A4
Observatory Rd.	60 B2
Maree Dr.	
Margaret St.	60 A2
Martha St.	
Marine Cres.	62 C2
Marine Gdns.	58 B2
Mariscat Rd.	56 C1
Market St.	57 A3
Markinch St.	58 A2
West St.	56 C1
Marlborough Av.	62 B1
Marlow St.	56 C1
Marlow Ter.	56 B1
Seaward St.	
Marmion St.	57 C4
Marne St.	59 B4
Mart St.	59 B3

Street	Pg/Ref
Martha St.	
Martin St.	60 A2
Martyr St.	61 C3
Marwick St.	
Mary St.	61 A4
Maryhill Rd.	64 C1
Maryland Dr.	63 B4
Maryland Gdns.	58 B1
Marywood Sq.	58 B1
Masterton St.	56 A2
Mathieson La.	64 B2
Mathieson St.	60 C2
Mathieson St.	
Matilda Rd.	60 C2
Mauchline St.	59 C4
Mauldslie St.	60 C1
Maule Dr.	61 C4
Mavisbank Gdns.	62 C2
Mavisbank La.	58 A2
Govan Rd.	
Maxwell Av.	59 C4
Maxwell Dr.	59 C3
Maxwell Gdns.	59 C3
Maxwell Gro.	59 C4
Maxwell Oval	60 C1
Maxwell Pl.	59 C4
Maxwell Rd.	59 C4
Maxwell Sq.	59 C4
Maxwell St.	60 B2
May Ter.	57 B3
Prospecthill Rd.	
Maybank La.	57 A3
Victoria Rd.	
Maybank St.	63 A4
Mayfield St.	60 B1
McAlpine St.	56 B1
McArthur St.	
Pleasance St.	56 B1
McAslin Ct.	60 A2
McAslin St.	61 A3
McCulloch St.	59 C4
McFarlane St.	61 B3
McGregor St.	58 B1
McIntosh Ct.	61 A3
McIntosh St.	
McIntosh St.	59 A4
McIntyre St.	61 A3
McLean Sq.	57 B3
McLennan St.	61 B3
McLeod St.	58 A1
McNeil St.	60 C2
McPhail St.	64 C1
McPhater St.	
Dunblane St.	60 B2
McPherson St.	58 A1
High St.	62 C2
Meadow Rd.	61 A4
Meadowpark St.	62 C1
Meadowside Quay	
Meadowside St.	62 C2
Megan Gate	61 C3
Megan St.	
Megan St.	61 C3
Melbourne St.	58 A1
Meldon Pl.	
Meldrum Gdns.	58 C2
Melfort Av.	58 B1
Melrose Gdns.	
Melrose St.	
Queens Cres.	63 A3
Melvaig Pl.	60 A2
Melville Ct.	
Brunswick St.	59 C4
Melville St.	65 A3
Memel St.	57 C3
Menock Rd.	65 A4
Menzies Dr.	65 A4
Menzies Pl.	60 B2
Menzies Rd.	
Merchant La.	
Clyde St.	
Merkland Ct.	62 C2
Vine St.	
Merkland St.	58 B2
Merrick Gdns.	56 C1
Merryburn Av.	57 A3
Merryland Pl.	58 A2
Merryland St.	56 C1
Merrylee Cres.	56 C1
Merrylee Rd.	56 B1
Merryvale Pl.	59 B4
Metropole La.	59 B3
Howard St.	
Midcroft Av.	57 C4
Middlesex St.	59 B4
Middleton St.	59 B3

60 B1	Midland St.
59 B3	Midlock St.
56 A1	Midlothian Dr.
65 B3	Midton St.
64 C2	Midwharf St.
63 A3	Migvie Pl.
	Wyndford Rd.
60 C1	Milan St.
61 C3	Mill Cres.
61 C3	Mill St.
65 B3	Millarbank St.
56 B2	Millbrae Ct.
	Millbrae Rd.
56 B2	Millbrae Cres.
56 B2	Millbrae Rd.
65 C4	Millburn St.
A2	Miller St.
61 C4	Millerfield Pl.
61 C4	Millerfield Rd.
61 B4	Millerston St.
61 B3	Millpond Dr.
57 B4	Millport Av.
61 B3	Millroad Dr.
61 B3	Millroad Gdns.
61 B3	Millroad St.
56 B2	Millwood St.
61 A4	Milnbank St.
62 A1	Milner Rd.
59 B4	Milnpark Gdns.
59 B4	Milnpark St.
64 C1	Milton St.
56 A2	Minard Rd.
59 A4	Minerva St.
59 A4	Minerva Way
63 B3	Mingarry La.
	Clouston St.
63 B4	Mingarry St.
58 B1	Minto Cres.
58 B1	Minto St.
64 A1	Mireton St.
63 B3	Mirrlees Dr.
63 B3	Mirrlees La.
	Redlands Rd.
60 A1	Mitchell La.
	Buchanan St.
60 A1	Mitchell St.
62 B1	Mitre Ct.
	Mitre Rd.
62 B1	Mitre La.
62 B1	Mitre La. W.
	Mitre La.
62 B1	Mitre Rd.
56 C2	Mochrum St.
60 C2	Moffat St.
58 B1	Moidart Cres.
	Moidart Rd.
58 B1	Moidart Pl.
	Moidart Rd.
58 B1	Moidart Rd.
60 B2	Moir La.
	Moir St.
60 B2	Moir St.
60 B2	Molendinar St.
65 B3	Mollinsburn St.
64 B1	Monar Dr.
64 B1	Monar Pl.
64 B1	Monar St.
63 B4	Monart Pl.
	Caithness St.
64 C1	Moncrieff St.
	North Woodside Rd.
64 C1	Moncrieff St.
	Braid Sq.
61 B3	Moncur St.
58 C1	Moness Dr.
62 C2	Monkscroft Av.
62 C2	Monkscroft Ct.
62 B2	Monkscroft Gdns.
	Monkscroft Av.
62 A2	Monmouth Av.
56 C1	Monreith Rd.
57 C3	Monreith Rd. E.
62 B2	Montague La.
62 B2	Montague St.
62 B2	Montague Ter.
	Hyndland Rd.
61 B3	Monteith Pl.
61 B3	Monteith Row
61 B3	Monteith Row La.
	Monteith Pl.
57 B4	Montford Av.
57 B3	Montgomery La.
	Somerville St.
61 C3	Montgomery St.
	London Rd.
60 A2	Montrose St.

60 B2	Moodies Ct.
	Osborne St.
61 B4	Moore St.
60 A2	Morar Rd.
58 B1	Morar Rd.
56 A2	Moray Pl.
60 B1	Moray Pl.
60 C1	Morgan Ms.
56 A2	Morley St.
65 B3	Morrin Path
56 A2	Morrin Sq.
	Collins St.
65 B3	Morrin St.
61 B3	Morris Pl.
60 B1	Morrison St.
60 A1	Morrisons Ct.
	Argyle St.
63 B4	Mortimer St.
	Hotspur St.
56 A1	Morton Gdns.
60 B1	Morven St.
65 A3	Mosesfield St.
65 A3	Mosesfield Ter.
	Balgrayhill Rd.
56 A1	Moss-side Rd.
56 C1	Mossgiel Rd.
58 C1	Mosspark Av.
58 C1	Mosspark Boul.
58 C1	Mosspark Oval
58 C1	Mosspark Sq.
57 B3	Mount Annan Dr.
56 B2	Mount St.
56 B2	Mount Stuart St.
61 B4	Mountainblue St.
63 C3	Moy St.
	Church St.
65 B3	Muir St.
62 C2	Muirhead St.
	Purdon St.
56 A2	Muirhouse St.
	Pollokshaws Rd.
62 C2	Muirpark St.
56 C2	Muirskeith Cres.
56 C2	Muirskeith Pl.
56 C2	Muirskeith Rd.
56 C1	Mulberry Rd.
65 C4	Mull St.
62 A1	Munro La.
62 A1	Munro Pl.
62 A1	Munro Rd.
63 B4	Murano St.
65 A3	Murdoch St.

N

60 C2	Naburn St.
63 C3	Nairn St.
61 B4	Nansen St.
58 A2	Napier Dr.
58 A2	Napier Pl.
58 A2	Napier Pl.
59 A3	Napier St.
58 A2	Napier Ter.
63 C4	Napiershall La.
	Napiershall St.
63 C4	Napiershall Pl.
	Napiershall St.
63 C4	Napiershall St.
62 B1	Naseby Av.
60 A1	National Bk. La.
	St. Vincent St.
60 A2	Nelson Mandela Pl.
	Buchanan St.
60 B1	Nelson St.
63 B4	Nelson Ter.
	Glasgow St.
63 B4	Neptune St.
59 C3	Netherby Dr.
60 B2	New City Rd.
60 B2	New Wynd
59 C3	Newark Dr.
57 C4	Newburgh St.
57 C4	Newcroft Dr.
61 C3	Newhall St.
56 B1	Newlands Rd.
	Newlandsfield Rd.
63 C4	Newton Pl.
59 A4	Newton Ter.
	Sauchiehall St.

63 C4	Newton Ter. La.
	Elderslie St.
60 A2	Nicholas St.
60 B1	Nicholson La.
	Nicholson St.
60 B1	Nicholson St.
56 A2	Niddrie Rd.
56 A2	Niddrie Sq.
56 A1	Nigel Gdns.
58 A1	Nimmo Dr.
56 A2	Nithsdale Dr.
59 C4	Nithsdale Pl.
	Shields Rd.
58 C2	Nithsdale St.
56 A2	Nithsdale St.
63 A3	Niven St.
62 B1	Norby Rd.
57 B3	Norfield Dr.
60 B1	Norfolk Ct.
60 B1	Norfolk La.
	Norfolk St.
60 B2	Norfolk St.
57 C3	Norham St.
56 C2	Norman St.
60 B1	North Canalbank St.
63 C4	North Claremont St.
63 C4	North Ct. La.
	Buchanan St.
60 B2	North Dr.
60 A2	North Frederick St.
62 B2	North Gardner St.
59 B3	North Gower St.
56 B2	North Hanover Pl.
56 B2	North Hanover St.
59 A4	North Pl.
	North St.
60 A2	North Portland St.
60 A2	North Queen St.
	George Sq.
64 C1	North Spiers Wf.
59 A4	North St.
64 C2	North Wallace St.
60 B1	North Woodside Rd.
62 A2	Northampton Dr.
62 A2	Northampton La.
	Northampton Dr.
65 B3	Northcroft Rd.
63 B4	Northpark St.
63 B4	Northpark Ter.
	Hamilton Dr.
63 B4	Northumberland St.
62 C2	Norval St.
63 C4	Norwich Dr.
63 C4	Norwood Ter.
	Southpark Av.
62 A2	Nottingham Av.
62 A2	Nottingham La.
	Northampton Dr.
62 B2	Novar Dr.
61 C4	Nuneaton St.
56 A2	Nursery La.
56 A2	Nursery St.
	Pollokshaws Rd.
56 A2	Nursery St. La.
	Nithsdale Dr.
57 A3	Nutberry Ct.

O

60 A1	Oak St.
	Cadogan St.
64 B1	Oakbank La.
59 B4	Oakbank Ter.
63 C4	Oakfield Av.
63 C4	Oakfield Ter.
	Oakfield Av.
60 B2	Oakley Ter.
65 B4	Oatfield St.
63 B4	Oban Ct.
63 B4	Oban Dr.
63 C3	Observatory La.
	Observatory Rd.
63 B3	Observatory Rd.
57 C3	Old Castle Rd.
61 C3	Old Dalmarnock Rd.
63 C3	Old Dumbarton Rd.
60 B1	Old Rutherglen Rd.
60 B2	Old Wynd
59 C4	Olrig Ter.
	Shields Rd.
61 B3	Olympia St.
61 A4	Onslow Dr.

61 A4	Onslow Sq.
	Onslow Dr.
63 A4	Oran Gdns.
63 A4	Oran Gate
63 A4	Oran Pl.
63 A4	Oran St.
57 C3	Orchy St.
60 C2	Oregon Pl.
58 A2	Orkney Pl.
	Orkney St.
65 B4	Orkney St.
58 A2	Orleans Av.
62 B1	Orleans La.
62 B1	Orr Pl.
61 B3	Orr St.
58 B2	Orton St.
65 B3	Orwell St.
58 B2	Osborn Ter.
	Copland Rd.
59 A4	Osborne St.
60 C2	Osborne Vill.
	Holmhead St.
64 B2	Ossian Rd.
61 C3	Oswald La.
	Oswald St.
60 A1	Oswald St.
59 B3	Otago La.
	Otago St.
59 B4	Otago La. N.
	Otago St.
63 C4	Otago St.
62 C2	Otter La.
	Castlebank St.
56 B2	Overdale Av.
56 B2	Overdale Gdns.
56 B2	Overdale St.
56 B2	Overdale Vills.
	Overdale St.
62 B2	Overnewton Pl.
	Kelvinhaugh St.
62 B2	Overnewton Sq.
58 B2	Overnewton St.
61 B4	Overtown St.
57 C4	Overwood Dr.
60 B1	Oxford La.
60 B1	Oxford St.

P

59 B4	Paisley Rd.
59 B2	Paisley Rd. W.
65 B3	Palermo St.
59 A3	Palmerston Pl.
	Kelvinhaugh St.
60 B1	Panmure St.
64 B1	Park Av.
64 B1	Park Circ.
63 C4	Park Circ. La.
	Lynedoch Pl.
62 B2	Park Circ. Pl.
63 B3	Park Dr.
63 C4	Park Gdns.
63 C4	Park Gdns. La.
	Clifton St.
62 B2	Park Gate
62 B2	Park La.
60 A2	Park Quad.
63 B3	Park Rd.
56 B1	Park St. S.
57 A4	Park Ter. (G3)
56 A2	Park Ter. (G42)
	Queens Dr.
62 C1	Parker St.
63 C4	Parkgrove Ter.
59 A4	Parkgrove Ter. La.
	Derby St.
56 B1	Parkhill Rd.
59 B4	Parkholm La.
	Paisley Rd.
61 A3	Parliament Rd.
60 B2	Parnie St.
61 A3	Parson St.
60 A2	Parsonage Row
60 A2	Parsonage Sq.
63 C3	Partick Bri. St.
62 B2	Partickhill Av.
62 B2	Partickhill Av.
	Partickhill Rd.
62 B2	Partickhill Rd.
63 B4	Paterson St.
61 A4	Patna St.
61 A4	Paton St.
60 B1	Payne St.
58 A2	Pearce St.
61 B3	Peathill St.
62 C2	Peel La.
	Burgh Hall St.
62 C2	Peel St.

59 A4	Pembroke St.
58 A1	Peninver Dr.
62 A2	Penrith Dr.
61 C3	Pentland Pl.
56 C1	Pentland Rd.
59 B3	Percy St.
59 A4	Perth St.
	Argyle St.
65 B4	Petershill Ct.
65 B4	Petershill Dr.
65 B4	Petershill Pl.
65 B4	Petershill Rd.
56 A1	Peveril Av.
64 C1	Phoenix Pk. Ter.
	Corn St.
64 C1	Phoenix St.
	Great Western Rd.
59 A4	Piccadilly St.
60 C2	Pine Pl.
64 B2	Pinkston Dr.
64 B2	Pinkston Rd.
61 C3	Pirn St.
60 A1	Pitt St.
59 B3	Plantation Pk. Gdns.
59 B4	Plantation Pl.
	Govan Rd.
59 B4	Plantation Sq.
61 C4	Playfair St.
56 B1	Pleasance La.
56 B1	Pleasance St.
56 A2	Pollokshaws Rd.
57 A4	Polmadie Av.
57 A4	Polmadie Rd.
57 A4	Polmadie St.
62 B2	Polwarth Gdns.
	Novar Dr.
62 B2	Polwarth La.
	Novar Dr.
62 B2	Polwarth St.
62 B1	Poplar Av.
62 B1	Poplar Rd.
	Urrdale Rd.
61 C3	Poplin St.
60 A2	Port Dundas Pl.
60 A2	Port Dundas Rd.
59 A4	Port St.
63 C4	Portman Pl.
	Cowan St.
59 B4	Portman St.
60 B1	Portugal La.
	Bedford St.
60 B1	Portugal St.
	Norfolk St.
64 B1	Possil Cross
64 B1	Possil Rd.
57 A3	Preston Pl.
62 B2	Prince Albert Rd.
57 C3	Prince Edward St.
63 B3	Prince of Wales Ter.
64 C1	Prince's Dock
62 B2	Princes Gdns.
62 B3	Princes Pl.
62 B3	Princes Sq.
62 B3	Princes St.
56 B1	Prospect Rd.
57 A4	Prospecthill Circ.
57 B4	Prospecthill Dr.
57 B3	Prospecthill Rd.
57 B4	Prospecthill Sq.
65 C3	Provanhill Pl.
62 C2	Purdon St.

Q

56 C2	Quadrant Rd.
60 A1	Queen Arc.
	Renfrew St.
60 C2	Queen Elizabeth Sq.
63 B4	Queen Margaret Ct.
63 B4	Queen Margaret Cres.
	Hamilton Dr.
63 B3	Queen Margaret Dr.
63 B4	Queen Margaret Rd.
57 A3	Queen Mary Av.
57 A3	Queen Mary St.
56 A2	Queen Sq.
60 A2	Queen St.
64 C1	Queens Cres.
63 B4	Queens Cross
56 A2	Queens Dr.

57 A3	Queens Dr. La.
63 B3	Queens Gdns.
	Victoria Cres. Rd.
57 A3	Queens Pk. Av.
63 B3	Queens Pl.
62 B2	Queensborough Gdns.
65 B3	Queenshill St.
56 A2	Quentin St.

R

59 A4	Radnor St.
	Argyle St.
63 B4	Raeberry St.
64 C1	Raglan St.
62 B1	Randolph Rd.
57 C3	Rannoch St.
58 A2	Ratford St.
58 A2	Rathlin St.
65 A3	Ratho Dr.
56 B1	Ravenshall Rd.
56 A1	Ravenswood Dr.
65 B4	Red Rd.
65 B4	Red Rd. Ct.
61 B3	Redan St.
63 B3	Redlands La.
	Kirklee Rd.
63 B3	Redlands Rd.
63 B3	Redlands Ter.
63 B3	Redlands Ter. La.
	Julian Av.
64 A1	Redmoss St.
64 B2	Rednock St.
65 B4	Redwood Dr.
	Foresthall Dr.
63 C3	Regent Moray St.
56 A2	Regent Pk. Sq.
56 A2	Regent Pk. Ter.
	Pollokshaws Rd.
56 B1	Regwood St.
61 C3	Reid Pl.
	Muslin St.
61 C3	Reid St.
65 B3	Reidhouse St.
	Muir St.
61 B3	Reidvale St.
60 A1	Renfield St.
60 A1	Renfrew Ct.
	Renfrew St.
60 A1	Renfrew La.
	Renfield St.
60 A1	Renfrew St.
64 C2	Renton St.
59 B4	Renwick St.
	Scotland St.
57 C3	Rhannan Rd.
57 C3	Rhannan Ter.
65 C3	Rhymer St.
58 B2	Rhynie Dr.
57 A4	Riccarton St.
60 A1	Richard St.
	Cadogan St.
60 A2	Richmond St.
61 B4	Rimsdale St.
63 B3	Ringford St.
62 A2	Ripon Dr.
61 B3	Risk St.
60 C1	Ritchie St.
56 B2	River Rd.
	Mansionhouse Rd.
56 B1	Riverbank St.
56 B1	Riverford Rd.
56 B2	Riverside Rd.
60 B1	Riverview Av.
	West St.
60 B1	Riverview Dr.
60 B1	Riverview Gdns.
60 B1	Riverview Pl.
65 B3	Robb St.
58 A2	Robert St.
56 A1	Roberton Av.
60 A1	Robertson La.
	Robertson St.
60 A1	Robertson St.
57 A3	Robson Gro.
64 B1	Rock St.
61 B4	Rockbank Pl.
	Broad St.
61 B4	Rockbank St.
61 C3	Rockcliffe St.
64 C1	Rodney St.
61 C4	Roebank St.
61 B3	Rogart St.
63 B3	Rokeby Ter.
	Great Western Rd.